Find Anyone FAST

By Phone, FAX, Mail And Computer

Richard S. Johnson

MIE Publishing

Find Anyone *FAST*
by Richard S. Johnson

Copyright © 1995 by Military Information Enterprises, Inc.

Published by:

MIE Publishing
PO Box 340081
San Antonio, TX 78234

MIE Publishing   (800) 937-2133
PO Box 5143
Burlington, North Carolina 27216

Library of Congress Cataloging in Publication Data
Johnson, Richard S., 1933-
Find Anyone Fast

Includes index.
ISBN 1-877639-20-6
1. Missing persons—United States—Investigation. I. Title.
HV6762.U5J64   1995   94-48632
362.8—dc20   CIP

Table Of Contents

About The Author

Richard (Dick) S. Johnson is a professional researcher. He has operated the Nationwide Locator, a computer locator service in San Antonio, Texas, since 1988. The author has personally solved thousands of difficult missing person cases involving relatives, birth parents, witnesses, heirs and debtors. He has made many family and military reunions possible. He has also solved many difficult cases for national and foreign media.

Dick Johnson is recognized as a national expert on locating missing people. Additionally, he is the foremost expert in the nation on locating people with a military connection.

He served 28 years in the military. For the last fifteen years of service, he was involved with personnel operations and commanded computer centers. He was responsible for the locator service for two large Army commands. Dick retired from the Army in 1979 as a Lieutenant Colonel, but his interest in locating people continued. For several years, he did extensive research on this subject. His expertise includes knowledge of records, manual search techniques as well as computer search techniques and databases.

The Salvation Army, the Veterans of Foreign Wars, the State Department, "Unsolved Mysteries", major libraries and researchers have referred people looking for individuals to Dick Johnson and his books.

Dick Johnson has appeared on hundreds of radio talk shows and numerous television programs to include "The Ricki Lake Show", "Company" and "Case Closed." He has also located numerous people for "The Crusaders", "Case Closed", "The Marilyn Connection", "The Elvis Connection" and many other national television programs as well as numerous magazines and newspapers.

The author has located people for television programs and newspapers in France, Belgium, Japan and Great Britain. He was featured in an article in the *AARP Bulletin*. Dick is a consultant on methods to find missing people and is often called upon by professional organizations to speak on this subject. He has also been a guest on America On-Line forums.

Dick is the author of "Searching", a column that appears in *The Stars and Stripes, The National Tribune* newspaper and *Reunions magazine*. This column discusses unique searches that he has solved which have a great deal of human interest

He is also the author of the book *How To Locate Anyone Who Is Or Has Been In The Military: Armed Forces Locator Guide*. The foreword to this book is by General William C. Westmoreland It has received favorable reviews from numerous national magazines and newspapers. Over 65,000 copies of this unique book have been sold. It is now in its sixth (1995) edition. It has helped thousands of people to locate literally thousands of people with military connections.

In this book, *Find Anyone Fast*, the author shares with you the wealth of knowledge, experience and professional secrets he has gained over numerous years of work and research. He has expended a great deal of effort to include as much useful and current information as possible. Of particular interest to individual searchers is the information included concerning computer databases and searches that are available.

Acknowledgement

It would be impossible to name all the people who have contributed information contained in this book. The list would include individuals who work for the federal government, libraries, professional searchers and numerous other individuals.

This book would not be possible without the dedicated and devoted work of Julie Delpho, Debbie Knox and Libby Lindsey. They have spent untold hours in the acquisition of information, editing, composing and formatting of this book.

Disclaimer

This book is designed to provide information about locating missing people. It is sold with the understanding that the publisher and author are not engaged in rendering legal or other professional services.

Every effort has been made to make this book as complete and accurate as possible. There may be mistakes, either typographical or in content. Therefore, this book should be used as a general guide and not the ultimate source of search material.

The purpose of this book is to educate on the subject matter. The author or MIE Publishing shall have neither liability nor responsibility to any person regarding any loss or damage caused or alleged to be caused directly or indirectly by the information contained in this book.

Preface

This book was written due to the great demand for accurate and useful information concerning locating missing people. There are numerous books that deal with this subject, but few of them are truly effective. This is because either the people who wrote these books are not actively involved with locating missing people or the information is not current.

There are a few laws that may restrict the information that is available. These will be discussed in more detail as specific searches and databases are explained. Examples of these laws include the **Freedom of Information Act**, the **Privacy Act** and the **Fair Credit Reporting Act**.

This book is intended for use by the general public, but may also be beneficial to private investigators, skip tracers, collection agencies, attorneys, reunion planners and others who need to find missing people. It will demonstrate in simple terms the methods and information needed to locate these individuals. All the methods described in this book are legal. This is not a book of "dirty tricks" or "deceptive tactics". Thousands of people have been located with the techniques and methods listed in this book.

Chapter One

How To Use This Book

In order to secure a quick and successful search, it is important to use the information provided in this book properly. Read this book all the way through. Some sections must be read several times to understand them completely.

Each chapter of this book deals with specific steps of searching. **Chapters Two** and **Three** discuss identifying information about the individual. **Chapter Four** explains the methods used to locate individuals. **Chapters Five** through **Eight** explain where to go for information and assistance in your search. **Chapter Nine** tells how to determine if the subject is deceased. Computer searches and databases are discussed in **Chapter Ten**. Finally, **Chapter Eleven** focuses on case histories and other useful information. Whenever possible, topics within each chapter are listed in alphabetical order. **Appendix A** explains where and when Social Security number are assigned. **Appendix B** is the format to be used when requesting information from the federal government or the armed forces under the provisions of the Freedom Of Information Act. **Appendix C** is a copy of the Standard Form 180 needed to acquire military records.

Since each person is unique, each search will be different. There are many ways to use this book. Tailor your search to the information available to you. Organize your effort and gather as much information as possible about your subject. This process will continue until you are successful.

Finally, use common sense and be persistent. Learn to be a good listener. Review your work from time to time and check everything previously tried. Do not be afraid to ask questions or to redo your work. Review this book again to be sure you did not miss any opportunity to find a lead. When hot on someone's trail, keep after them while the information is fresh. Remember, most people are easy to locate. The rest can ultimately be located if you are positive, persistent, patient and polite.

The following abbreviations are used throughout this book:

ATTN	Attention
DMV	Department of Motor Vehicles
DOB	date of birth
DOD	date of death
DPS	Department of Public Safety
FOIA	Freedom of Information Act
IRS	Internal Revenue Service
MVR	Motor Vehicle Registration
NPRC	National Personnel Records Center
SSA	Social Security Administration
SSN	Social Security number
USA	US Army
USAF	US Air Force
USCG	US Coast Guard
USMC	US Marine Corps
USN	US Navy
VA	Department of Veterans Affairs
YOB	year of birth

Few people in this country actually qualify as "missing". This only occurs when a family member notifies the police that someone is "missing." However, that is not always the case.

Most missing people are not, in fact "missing" at all. They have simply moved and we do not know their current whereabouts. We live in a highly mobile society and this is a common situation. People move when they have a new job, enter the military, are transferred by their employer, the military, divorce, change schools, retire, purchase a new house or rent a new apartment.

Contrary to what almost everyone believes, most people can be found with very little effort and a small amount of time and money. Some cases may take more time and effort than others, but there are very few people who cannot be located. This is especially true today because there is a great deal of important information in public records and numerous national databases available that anyone can access to find anyone fast!

Who is looking for these "missing" people? Answers vary with each case, but most are being sought by:

- their family
- birth children in search of their natural parents
- old lovers, old friends, military buddies
- school, family and military reunions, groups and associations
- high school and college alumni groups
- civic, patriotic, veterans, and historical organizations
- genealogical researchers
- former spouses who are due alimony and child support
- people who are owed money

- searchers for missing heirs to estates
- state agencies and businesses who hold abandoned money and assets
- people seeking the owners of oil and mineral rights
- people seeking the owners of real estate or property they wish to purchase
- attorneys seeking witnesses for court cases
- law enforcement agencies seeking fugitives
- federal, state and county agencies who are due taxes
- medical agencies and organizations in need of medical information or other important data
- businesses attempting to update their mailing lists
- numerous other people and organizations

No matter who you are or who you are looking for, with the methods in this book, you can -- Find Anyone *FAST* !

Chapter Two

Gathering Information About The Individual

The first step in your search is to obtain as much identifying information as possible about the subject. **Identifying information** is the data that makes a person unique. Examples of identifying information are a person's Social Security number, date of birth and physical description. Other examples are names of relatives, places of employment and membership in social, professional and other organizations. The more information you obtain on the person, the easier it will be to find him or her.

It is extremely important that you are as organized as possible. Record all identifying information on the **Individual Data Worksheet** (located at the end of this chapter), in a notebook or a computer file. Keep all the information together and write or type neatly so you can read and understand your notes later. Record all new information as soon as you obtain it and it is fresh in your memory.

The process of obtaining identifying information is a continual one that goes on until you locate your subject. This means whenever you obtain any identifying information, it must be recorded immediately. The reason for this is obvious, as no one can remember every bit of information collected. You must be able to review this information frequently, so it must be clearly written or recorded. If you fail to do this, you will end up redoing a lot of research needlessly or you may become frustrated in your search.

The following categories are examples of identifying information that should be obtained and recorded:

Names - complete legal name (first, middle and last or surname), nicknames, maiden name, previous married names, and aliases

Personal Identifying information - Social Security number, date and place of birth, driver license numbers, physical description (height, weight, color of hair and eyes, tattoos, scars, pictures, disabilities, etc.)

Personal credit history - credit history and bankruptcy information

Criminal history - traffic violations, jail and prison records, record of arrests

Names and addresses of relatives and friends - names of parents, spouses, former spouses, brothers and sisters, other relatives (aunts, uncles, cousins, etc.), children, children's spouses, if married, and their addresses and telephone numbers (home and work)

Military information - service number, VA claim number, VA insurance number, military service branch, dates of military service, units or ships assigned, installations or bases assigned, assignments in Vietnam, Korea, etc., rank or rating (if not known, whether an officer or enlisted), disability, membership in veteran and military reunion organizations, membership in the reserve or National Guard / units / dates of assignments

Property owned - real estate, automobiles, boats, motorcycles and guns owned and state in which registered

Schools attended - elementary, high school, colleges and universities attended and dates, subjects studied, college majors and degrees received

Employment related information - previous employment, labor union membership, professional membership, names and addresses of former employers and fellow employees

Social history - church or synagogue affiliation, membership in lodges, fraternal and service organization, names, addresses and telephone numbers of friends, political party affiliation and voter registration information, foreign and national travel history

Avocations and hobbies - talents, stamp collecting, athletics, hunting, boating, fishing, pilot, amateur radio and motorcycle riding, etc.

Lifestyle information - drinking habits, drug use, civic activities, religious activities, type of friends, etc.

The value of the above information will be discussed in greater detail throughout this book.

It cannot be overemphasized, the more information you can obtain about your subject, the easier it will be to find him or her. Numerous sources of information are available to help locate the missing person. Some examples of these sources are: family, friends, neighbors, former employers and employees, social organizations, schools and colleges, alumni groups, veterans organizations, churches, libraries, federal, state and local government agencies, and numerous computer databases. These sources of identifying information are discussed in greater detail throughout the book.

In order to work your case efficiently and effectively, it is essential to maintain an **Individual Data Worksheet**. This worksheet will keep you on track if you immediately and consistently enter the information on it as it is received and/or learned. The worksheet will also remind you of the ground you have covered and where you must go to obtain answers to outstanding questions or missing information.

The following information should be included on the **Individual Data Worksheet** you prepare.

Individual Data Worksheet

Complete legal name, nick names, maiden name, previous
married names, and aliases: _____

_____

Social Security number: _____

Date of birth: _____

Place of birth: _____

Parents' names: _____

_____

Spouse and former spouse's name: _____

_____

Names of brothers and sisters: _____

_____

Names of other relatives: _____

_____

Children's names and addresses: _____

_____

Previous addresses: _____

_____

_____

Previous telephone number: _____

Military service number: _____

VA claim number/VA insurance number: _____

Branch of military service: _____

Dates of military service: _____

Unit or ship assigned: _____

Installation or base assigned: _____

Assignments in Vietnam, Korea, etc.: _____

_____

Rank or rating (if not known, officer or enlisted): _____

_____

Membership in veterans and military reunion organizations:

_____

Membership in the reserve or National Guard units/dates of assignment: _____

_____

Real estate owned: _____

Automobiles, motorcycles and boats owned/state in which registered: _____

Elementary, high schools, colleges and universities attended, locations and dates: _____

_____

Previous employment/dates and locations: _____

_____

Church or synagogue affiliation: _____

Union membership: _____

Professional membership/licenses: _____

_____

Lodges, fraternal and service organization membership:

_____

Physical description: height, weight, color of hair and eyes, tattoos, scars, etc. (obtain photos): _____

_____

Hunting, boating or fishing licenses: _____

Pilot, amateur radio, driver and motorcycle licenses:

_____

Names, addresses and telephone numbers of friends and fellow employees: _____

_____

Hobbies, talents and avocations: _____

Political party affiliation and voter's registration: _____

_____

Foreign and national travel history: _____

_____

Dates and places of bankruptcy: _____

Miscellaneous information: _____

Chapter Three

The Individual's Name

The most important identifying information in any search is the name of the individual being sought. Many people are known by their nickname or their initials rather than their given name. Most government and public documents, such as real estate documents, tax lists, driver licenses, and military records, list the complete legal name. Government agencies that record the complete legal name are the **Social Security Administration**, the **Internal Revenue Service** and the **Department of Veterans Affairs**.

Do not assume that you know the person's complete, legal name. Verify what you have against public documents or government records whenever possible. Many people use their middle name as their first name such as former vice-president Dan Quayle, (his legal name is James Danforth Quayle). Some people may use an initial, their middle name, and their last name, such as "R. Stanley Smith". Also, some people legally change their name. Most women take their husband's surname upon marriage. Some, even though married, never take their husband's surname. They retain their maiden name or mix the two, such as "Mary Miles-Jones". These type of cases can be solved, especially if a Social Security number, a military service number or a date of birth is obtained. These identifying items do not change.

Keep in mind that a person's name is often entered into public records with incorrect spelling, e.g., "John Smithe," instead of "John Smith". The middle initial can be omitted. This type of error is more common than most people realize. Also, be aware that Junior (Jr.), Senior (Sr.), II, or III, may be used or omitted. This situation can cause problems with identification.

Check spelling variations of the name when reviewing records or databases. If you are not sure of the exact spelling of someone's surname, there are several books at most main libraries that deal with surnames and their alternate spellings. Some versions of the **National Telephone Directory** on CD ROM list alternate spellings for surnames. Telephone books will also have this information.

Hispanic and other ethnic groups often have hyphenated surnames. This may be a problem in a search. Most records and databases throughout the country were not set up to handle hyphenated names. Check for both names when searching records and files.

Women are usually more difficult to locate than men because they usually use their husband's surname when they marry. With a woman's SSN, you can locate her easily and find out her surname if she has married. Sometimes it is easier to find a woman by first finding her husband or her former spouse, if they are now divorced. Former spouses usually know an address, especially if they have children. In some cases, it may be easier to locate the person through their parents, siblings or their children.

Computer Social Security number traces will sometimes show maiden names and later entries will show the person's married name. The information on these databases is usually not over ten years old. VA computer files normally list both maiden name and married name for female veterans.

State driver license databases will often list women's maiden names, in addition to their married names.

People have been located with as little information as a first name or last name only, particularly if the name is uncommon. Of course, some other identifying information is needed, such as service in a particular unit in the military, date of birth, attendance at a particular school, etc. The **Date of Birth search** can provide the address of a person with only a last name and date of birth, or only a first name and date of birth. See **Chapter Ten** for details. Any search will be much easier if the individual's correct legal name is known. Even if you cannot find out a person's middle name, an initial will be a definite advantage in your search.

The following are sources to determine someone's legal name: **birth records, driver and MVR records** and **divorce records**. This information may also be obtained from churches, high school and college records, alumni associations, the VA, county and city tax offices, social clubs, and veterans organizations. Do not forget family, friends and former employers as a source for determining a legal name. Keep in mind that numerous people may use a nickname. This may be a common practice but their telephone numbers are usually listed under their legal names.

Again, any search will go faster if the correct full legal name of the person if known. Do everything possible to obtain this essential identifying information.

Chapter Four

Methods Of
Locating People

There are many ways of locating people. The methods vary depending upon the identifying information you have. It is possible to locate someone with:

- Name and Social Security number
- Name and date of birth
- Name and a former address
- Name and military service information
- Name and name of someone who knew them
- Name only

Locating People Using A Name and Social Security Number

Almost everyone in this country and its territories has a Social Security number (the abbreviation SSN is used throughout this book). While there is no law requiring a person to have one, you must have one to get a job, obtain credit, receive Social Security benefits or pay your federal income and Social Security taxes. Even children need a SSN to be claimed as dependents on federal income tax returns. Many states require a SSN to get a driver license and to pay state income taxes. Everyone entering the military must have a SSN, which replaced the military service number over 20 years ago. So in reality, it is extremely difficult to function in our society without a Social Security number.

Next to a person's name, the SSN is the single most important item in locating an individual. It is much easier to locate someone with their SSN than without it. But if you do not have an SSN, the person can still be located.

With a SSN computer trace against a credit database, 87 to 95 percent of people can be located quickly. A credit database is made up of credit files. Everyone who uses credit has a credit file. A credit file is updated each time a person uses credit to buy a house or a car, rent an apartment, or make any purchase using a credit card. A credit file can contain a person's full name, SSN, age or date or year of birth, current address, former address, dates addresses were reported, credit history and sometimes employer and name of spouse. Everything but the credit history is "header information" (see **Chapter Ten**). When a SSN trace is run, only this header information is given. The **Fair Credit Reporting Act** prohibits obtaining credit history information except for authorized reasons. Locating people is never considered an acceptable reason to access credit history.

Sometimes when a SSN trace is run, the name and SSN are checked by the computer against the SSA Master Death Index. If the individual is on this index, their date of death will be listed on the SSN trace.

There are three credit bureaus: **Trans Union, CBI-Equifax** and **TRW**. Each of these bureaus has its own credit database. These three bureaus combined have over 300 million individual credit files. Some people have files in one or two, and occasionally, all three of these credit bureaus. These credit databases are the most valuable resources in locating anyone. They are frequently used by collection agencies, private investigators and many reunion and alumni organizations. These groups usually gain access through a local dealer or a credit reporting agency in their community. A private individual must contact a locator service or a private investigator for this information. The retail price is usually around $30.00 to $65.00 to search one credit database. A search of all three credit databases can cost between $60.00 and $125.00.

Searches of federal and state records are easier to accomplish with an individual's SSN. The SSA files, VA files, many state driver license files and IRS files are some examples of government files that may be accessed with a SSN.

Sometimes women cannot be found through SSN searches because they marry and use their husband's credit. Therefore all credit information is reported with his SSN and not hers.

If you do not know the person's SSN, you should contact the following in order to obtain it:

- family members
- bank statements
- credit reports
- former employers
- income tax returns
- military records
- military orders and discharges
- military officers registers (1968-1978)
- old checks
- return addresses on letters from people who were or are in the military
- SSA records and correspondence

- college and university records
- driver license files
- some stocks and bonds
- mutual funds
- money market funds
- certificates of deposit
- voter registration files and letters from the VA

> VA claim numbers issued since 1973 consist of the individual's SSN with the letter "C" in front of the number.
>
> Sixteen states currently use the Social Security number as their driver license number.

The federal government is not allowed to release an individual's SSN because of the **Privacy Act**. Contrary to what many people believe, this law does not apply to state governments, businesses, private organizations or individuals. Individual states have their own privacy laws, but few are very restrictive.

A Social Security number is a tremendous asset for locating an individual. Time spent in finding this number is well worth the effort. Do not be afraid to ask anyone who may know the SSN of your subject. Do everything you can to obtain the individual's SSN. But remember to keep in mind that if the search is for the "current location" of the subject, do not become obsessed with obtaining their SSN.

Additional information on when and where SSN were issued is located in **Appendix A**.

Locating People Using A Name And Date Of Birth

The **date of birth** (DOB) is the next most important piece of identifying information, after the name and SSN, for locating an individual. Most government records of individuals include, as a minimum, the name and date of birth. Examples of this are driver licenses, military personnel records, VA records, divorce decrees, marriage licenses, birth and death certificates, voter registration files, and draft registration records.

You can obtain a person's current reported address or have a letter forwarded, using a name and a date of birth, from:

1. **Computer searches against credit file information:** some computer programs can access header information of credit files with name, DOB and a former address. See **Chapter Ten** for additional information.

2. **The Social Security Administration (SSA):** the SSA can identify an individual with a name and date of birth (or a SSN). Because of the Privacy Act, the SSA will not disclose an address or a Social Security number. They will verify if they have a death report of an individual, or if the individual has a SSN. They will also forward a letter to the person you are trying to contact (see **Chapter Five** for complete details).

3. **The Department of Veterans Affairs (VA):** the VA can usually identify a veteran with a name and DOB. Because of the Privacy Act they cannot give you the veteran's address. They will forward a letter if they have an address in their files (see **Chapter Five** for details).

You can obtain an individual's date of birth from:

- birth certificates
- church records
- criminal history records
- family members
- former employers
- former fellow employees
- friends
- insurance policies
- marriage licenses
- military personnel records
- school records
- draft registration records
- state drivers' records
- voter registration records
- Department of Veterans Affairs files
- social organizations
- professional organizations
- state licensing agencies

The Date of Birth search can search several national databases which contain millions of names and DOB. This search can provide current and former addresses of millions of people. See **Chapter Ten** for details.

Knowing the year of birth or even an estimated year of birth will assist you in securing the actual date of birth. Keep in mind that after the name and Social Security number, an individual's DOB is the most important piece of identifying information. Do everything possible to determine the individual's correct DOB. But remember that a subject can be located without a DOB.

Locating People Using A Former Address

A former address is an excellent means to locate an individual. With this information, no matter how old the address is, it is possible to track the person to their current address.

With the aid of old and current city directories, criss-cross directories and telephone books, an individual can be tracked from the last known address to a current one. If the trail ends before you find the current address, former neighbors can be contacted to find out when and where the person moved. With this new information, the search for appropriate city directories and telephone directories can resume.

Computer address updates (subject and address verification searches) may be used if the old addresses are not over ten years old. In many cases, the National DOB search can also provide former addresses as well as a DOB. See **Chapter Ten** for additional information on these computer searches.

Sources for obtaining former (or sometimes current) addresses are real estate and tax records, utility records, old telephone books, old city directories, voter registration records, professional licenses, hunting and fishing licenses, churches, schools and colleges, alumni associations, family, friends, former employers, former co-workers, military records, driver license files, motor vehicle registration files, social and veterans organizations, etc.

Since former addresses are such a valuable means of locating someone, it is important to contact as many people and organizations as possible in order to obtain a former address. This effort will speed up your search.

Locating People Using Military Service Information

There are 27 million living veterans in the Unites States. An individual who served in the armed forces may be located with any of the following information:

- Social Security number
- Military service number
- VA claim number
- Unit or ship the veteran was assigned
- Name and DOB
- Branch and date of service

The armed forces operate locator services to locate active, reserve and retired service members. This service is available to the public. The VA will forward a letter to veterans who are listed in their computer files. The **National Personnel Records Center** will provide copies of military records and in some cases forward letters to veterans. Military reunion groups and veterans organizations will either provide an address or forward a letter to veterans who are members of their organizations. More detailed information on this subject is provided in the latter chapters of this book.

Locating An Individual Through Someone Who Knew Them

People can often be easily located by contacting those who knew the subject. This fact is obvious, but it is often overlooked by even the best searchers.

The people and places to look for someone who knows or knew a subject are:

- family members
- former spouses, in-laws and step-children
- friends
- former neighbors
- former employers and co-workers
- schools, colleges and universities
- school and college reunion groups
- churches and religious organizations
- members of social organizations
- businesses where the subject received goods and services
- veterans organizations
- political organizations
- professional organizations

In most cases, a family member (father, mother, brother, sister, former spouse) will know the location of the individual. They may not know the street address, but they usually know the city where the person lives. They may also know the person's telephone number, DOB, SSN, church affiliation, political party membership, location of children and former spouse, reason for moving, etc. The same is true for many friends and social organizations and their members. Family members may also have old correspondence belonging to the subject that may list the SSN or an old address. This correspondence could be from the VA, banks, the military or the IRS.

Former neighbors are excellent sources for obtaining information about your subject's current location. However, many searchers often fail to use this valuable source. Find out where your subject last lived and either visit or call his neighbors and ask them if they have any information that will help you. Even if these people do not know the person's current location, they can probably give you the name of someone who does or other valuable clues.

Another useful source of information is to contact a place of business your subject frequented. The owner or manager may know your subject's new address or at least the city or state. Examples are:

- bars
- attorneys
- CPAs and tax preparers
- cleaners and launderers
- clothing stores
- grocery stores
- health spas
- convenience stores
- gas stations
- liquor stores
- auto repair shops
- restaurants
- travel agencies

You may want to contact the previous employers of your subject. Businesses usually know the forwarding address of former employees. If their personnel office does not know or will not provide an address, some of the former co-workers may know the individual's location. They usually know the reason a person left a job. Co-workers may know some information about your subject's personal life (i.e., divorce, retirement, new job, transfers, medical problems, name of spouse, children, ex-spouse, family problems, etc.) Employers should have SSN and DOB on file; be sure to ask for these identifying items.

Churches, synagogues, social and veterans' clubs may have records showing where the individual moved. If not, people who are members of these groups will have clues to a current location.

High schools and colleges usually have reunion or alumni associations that have most former students' addresses. Many publish directories of former students or keep mailing lists. In the event you cannot discover the address of the subject, you may be able to do so for some of his or her classmates. By contacting them, you may find the subject's current address.

There are thousands of employment and professional associations such as the **American Medical Association, American Nursing Association, American Bar Association, AFL-CIO**, etc. They often have national and local offices that can help. These organizations can provide addresses and, in some cases, the SSN and DOB. Be sure to ask for this information.

All of the sources discussed in this chapter can provide some of the following information:

- DOB
- SSN
- current location and telephone number
- location of children and former spouses
- why the subject moved
- if they had trouble with the law
- profession

- avocations
- description of vehicle
- memberships in church
- civic organizations
- hobbies
- schools and colleges attended and alumni groups

> **Note:** It is extremely important that you read **Chapter Ten** thoroughly. It will provide numerous methods to complete your search.

Locating People Using A Name Only

The more common the name, the more difficult it is to locate a person. Conversely, the less common the name (first or last) the easier it is to locate the person.

If a person's name is unique, it can sometimes be matched on VA files (if a veteran), some military locators (if on active duty), and some state driver license and state motor vehicle registration (MVR) offices. If you have the complete name, to include the middle initial, the chances of success are even greater.

The most common ways to obtain addresses are with the use of:

- The National Telephone Directory (CD ROM)
- Telephone books
- City directories
- Computer surname files
- CompuServe
- Date of birth search

Most of the above computer and CD-ROM searches will provide lists of names, addresses and listed telephone numbers that match the name of the person for whom you are looking. Again, the more common the name, the more matching addresses and phone numbers on the list. You might have a lot of letters to write or telephone calls to make in order to locate your subject. Normally, this is not the most desirable way to find someone. However, if the name is all you have (and you are unable to find any other clues to the subject's location), this method must be used.

If you do have some additional information about your subject, such as city or state of residence, the search can be narrowed down. The same is true if you have a DOB or a YOB, particularly with use of the National DOB search.

You should read Chapter Ten carefully, particularly if all the information you have on your subject is his or her name.

Chapter Five

Where To Obtain Information And Assistance From The Federal Government And The Armed Forces

It is possible to obtain identifying information and to locate individuals through federal government agencies and the armed forces.

Department Of Defense

The following section describes the ways to locate members of the armed forces who are on active duty or who have retired from the military.

Locate Active Duty And Retired Military Through Armed Forces World-Wide Locators

The armed forces world-wide locators will either forward a letter or provide the individual's current military unit of assignment. The latter may be limited to assignments in the United States.

To have a letter forwarded, place the letter in a sealed, stamped envelope. Put your name and return address in the upper left hand corner. In the center of the envelope put the rank, full name of the service member, followed by the SSN or DOB (if known). On a separate sheet of paper, list everything you know that may help the military locator identify the individual. For example:

- Name
- Rank
- Social Security number
- Military service e.g., active Air Force
- Date of birth (estimated if actual is unknown)
- Sex
- Officer or enlisted (if you are not sure of the rank)
- Date entered service
- Last assignment (if known)

In another envelope, preferably legal size, enclose the letter to be forwarded along with the fact sheet and a check for the search fee. The current search fee for all branches of the armed forces is $3.50, unless noted otherwise. Make check payable to Treasurer of the US. There is no search fee for military members or their immediate family. If this applies to you, state this on the fact sheet. On the outer envelope, include your name and return address. Address the envelope to the appropriate locator listed below.

If the military locator can identify the individual, it will forward your letter. It is then up to the individual to reply to your letter. If the military locator cannot forward the letter, it will return your letter and tell you why, e.g., discharged, retired, deceased or unable to identify.

To determine the unit and military base a person is assigned, write a letter to the appropriate locator listed below.

Include the search fee and as much information as possible to assist in identifying the person (as shown above).

Locate Active Duty, Reserve, National Guard Or Retired Air Force Personnel

Include a self-addressed stamped envelope with request for unit assignment and mail to: (the Air Force World-Wide locator will not provide overseas unit of assignment of active members)

USAF World-Wide Locator   Recording (210) 652-5774
AFMPC-RMIQL   (210) 652-5775
55 C Street West, Suite 50
Randolph AFB, TX 78150-4752

Locate Active Duty Army Personnel

This locator furnishes military addresses for individuals currently serving on active duty in the Army and for Department of the Army civilians. List the individual's full name, SSN or DOB. No information will be provided without these items. Mail request with a check or money order for $3.50 (no cash) for each name submitted. Checks should be made payable to "Finance Officer". Allow seven to ten working days for a reply. The locator keeps separation data for two years after a soldier is discharged or retired (date and place of discharge).

World-Wide Locator   Recording (317) 542-4211
US Army Enlisted Records
   and Evaluation Center
Ft. Benjamin Harrison, IN 46249-5301
$3.50 search fee.

Locate Retired Army Personnel

Army Reserve Personnel Center   (314) 538-3798
ATTN: DARP-VSE-VS
9700 Page Blvd.
St. Louis, MO 63132-5200
No fee charged.

Locate Active Duty Marine Corps Personnel

US Marine Corps-CMC   (703) 640-3942
(MMSB-10)
2008 Elliot Road, Room 201
Quantico, VA 22134-5030
$3.50 search fee.

Located Retired Marine Corps Personnel

Commandant of Marine Corps   (703) 614-1901
MMSR-6, Headquarters MC   FAX (703) 614-4400
#2 Navy Annex
Washington, DC 20380-1775
No search fee.

Locate Active Duty Navy Personnel

Bureau of Naval Personnel   (703) 614-3155
P-02116   (703) 614-5011
#2 Navy Annex   FAX (703) 614-1261
Washington, DC 20370-0210
* *This locator will only forward letters. The fee is $3.50.*

Locate Retired Navy Personnel

Navy Reserve Personnel Center   (800) 535-2699
4400 Dauphine Street   SSN 0-49 (504) 678-5400
New Orleans, LA 70149-7800   SSN 40-99 (504) 678-5434
money order $3.50 fee.   FAX (504) 942-6934

Locate Active Duty Military Through Base Locators

If you know the military base to which the individual is assigned, call directly to the base telephone operator or the base locator. You can mail a letter to the individual in care of the base locator. You do not need the individual's SSN or DOB to use the services of base locators. There is no fee charged for their service.

Locate People In The Military Prison

To determine if a former military member is or has been imprisoned in the US Disciplinary Barracks (military prison) at Ft. Leavenworth, Kansas, call **(913) 684-4629**. Approximately 1,500 inmates of all branches of the service are currently incarcerated. The prison keeps records of former inmates for up to ten years. Surname searches may be completed without date of birth or Social Security number.

Department Of Justice

Locate People In Federal Prisons

If the individual you are looking for (aliases may be available) may be in a federal prison, telephone the US prison federal locator at **(202) 307-3126**. Most prison locators keep records of former inmates for up to ten years. Surname searches may be completed without a date of birth or a Social Security number.

Immigration And Naturalization Service

The Immigration and Naturalization Service (INS) has duplicate records of all naturalizations that occurred after

September 26, 1906. Inquiries about citizenship granted after that date should be sent to the INS on a form that can be obtained from any of the INS district offices. Local postmasters can provide the address of the nearest district office or check your telephone book. For additional information, write to:

Immigration and Naturalization Service   (202) 514-4316
US Department of Justice
425 I Street, NW
Washington, DC 20536

Department Of State

Locate People Traveling Overseas

To locate US citizens traveling abroad, call the State Department's Citizens Emergency Center at **(202) 647-5225**.

Obtain Passport Application Records

Requests for information from passport records for US citizens after 1926 should be addressed to:

Passport Office
Department of State
Washington, DC 20520

Department Of Veterans Affairs

Locate Veterans Through The VA

The **Department of Veterans Affairs (VA)** will forward a letter in a similar manner as the armed forces. There are over 27 million living veterans. The VA does not have addresses for all veterans listed in their files. Only those who have applied for or are currently receiving VA benefits are listed. The address in their file is the address given when the veteran last obtained or applied for VA benefits. If the veteran is receiving VA benefits then the address will be current.

To have a letter forwarded, place it in an unsealed, stamped envelope with no return address. Put the veteran's name and VA claim number (or SSN if known) on the front of the envelope. Prepare a short fact sheet and state that you request the VA forward this letter to the veteran. Include all other pertinent information to ensure they can identify the veteran. Include as much information as possible such as: name, service number, SSN, DOB, branch of service, VA claim number, etc. Next, place this letter and the fact sheet in a larger envelope and mail to any **VA Regional Office**. If they cannot identify the individual, they will return your letter. The VA will inform you if the letter is undeliverable by the post office.

For additional information, contact the nearest VA Regional Office by dialing **(800) 827-1000**. You will be automatically connected with the VA Regional Office closest to you. You may contact the appropriate VA Regional Office through the addresses and telephone numbers listed below.

ALABAMA
VA Regional Office
345 Perry Hill Rd
Montgomery, AL 36109
(334) 279-4866

ALASKA
VA Regional Office
2925 Debarr Rd
Anchorage, AK 99508-2989
(907) 257-4700

ARIZONA
VA Regional Office
3225 N Central Ave
Phoenix, AZ 85012
(602) 263-5411

ARKANSAS
VA Regional Office
Bldg 65 Ft Roots
N Little Rock, AR 72115
(501) 370-3800

CALIFORNIA
VA Regional Office
11000 Wilshire Blvd
Los Angeles, CA 90024
(213) 479-4011

CALIFORNIA
VA Regional Office
2022 Camino Del Rio N
San Diego, CA 92108
(619) 297-8220

CALIFORNIA
VA Regional Office
1301 Clay St.
Oakland, CA 94612
(510) 637-1365

COLORADO
VA Regional Office
44 Union Blvd
Denver, CO 80225
(303) 980-1300

CONNECTICUT
VA Regional Office
450 Main St.
Hartford, CT 06103
(203) 278-3230

DELAWARE
VA Regional Office
1601 Kirkwood Hwy
Wilmington, DE 19805
(302) 998-0191

DISTRICT OF COLUMBIA
VA Regional Office
1120 Vermont Ave NW
Washington, DC 20421
(202) 418-4343

FLORIDA
VA Regional Office
144 1st Ave S
St Petersburg, FL 33701
(813) 898-2121

GEORGIA
VA Regional Office
730 Peachtree St NE
Atlanta, GA 30365
(404) 881-1776

HAWAII
VA Regional Office
300 Ala Moana Blvd
Honolulu, HI 96850
(808) 566-1000

IDAHO
VA Regional Office
805 W Franklin St
Boise, ID 83702
(208) 334-1010

ILLINOIS
VA Regional Office
536 S Clark St
Chicago, IL 60680
(312) 663-5510

INDIANA
VA Regional Office
575 N Pennsylvania St
Indianapolis, IN 46202
(317) 226-5566

IOWA
VA Regional Office
210 Walnut St
Des Moines, IA 50309
(515) 284-0219

KANSAS
VA Regional Office
5500 E Kellogg
Wichita, KS 67218
(316) 682-2301

KENTUCKY
VA Regional Office
545 S Third St
Louisville, KY 40202
(502) 584-2231

LOUISIANA
VA Regional Office
701 Loyola Ave
New Orleans, LA 70113
(504) 589-7191

MAINE
VA Regional Office
Rte 17 E
Togus, ME 04330
(207) 623-8000

MARYLAND
VA Regional Office
31 Hopkins Plaza
Baltimore, MD 21201
(410) 685-5454

MASSACHUSETTS
VA Regional Office
JFK Fed Bldg Gov Cen
Boston, MA 02203
(617) 227-4600

MICHIGAN
VA Regional Office
477 Michigan Ave
Detroit, MI 48226
(313) 964-5110

MINNESOTA
VA Regional Office
Fed Bldg Ft Snelling
St Paul, MN 55111
(612) 726-1454

MISSISSIPPI
VA Regional Office
100 W Capitol St
Jackson, MS 39269
(601) 965-4873

MISSOURI
VA Regional Office
400 South 18th St
St Louis, MO 63103
(314) 342-1171

MONTANA
VA Regional Office
Williams St & Hwy 12W
Ft Harrison, MT 59636
(406) 447-7975

NEBRASKA
VA Regional Office
5631 S 48th St
Lincoln, NE 68516
(402) 437-5001

NEVADA
VA Regional Office
1201 Terminal Way
Reno, NV 89520
(702) 329-9244

NEW HAMPSHIRE
VA Regional Office
275 Chestnut St
Manchester, NH 03101
(603) 666-7785

NEW JERSEY
VA Regional Office
20 Washington Pl
Newark, NJ 07102
(201) 645-2150

NEW MEXICO
VA Regional Office
500 Gold Ave SW
Albuquerque, NM 87102
(505) 766-3361

NEW YORK
VA Regional Office
111 W Huron St
Buffalo, NY 14202
(716) 551-5191

NEW YORK
VA Regional Office
245 W Houston St
New York, NY 10001
(212) 807-7229

NORTH CAROLINA
VA Regional Office
251 N Main Street
Winston-Salem, NC 27155
(919) 748-1800

NORTH DAKOTA
VA Regional Office
2101 Elm St
Fargo, ND 58102
(701) 293-3656

OHIO
VA Regional Office
1240 E 9th St
Cleveland, OH 44199
(216) 621-5050

OREGON
VA Regional Office
1220 SW 3rd Ave
Portland, OR 97204
(503) 221-2431

PENNSYLVANIA
VA Regional Office
1000 Liberty Ave
Pittsburgh, PA 15222
(412) 281-4233

PUERTO RICO
VA Regional Office
GPO Box 4867
San Juan, PR 00936
(809) 766-5141

SOUTH CAROLINA
VA Regional Office
1801 Assembly St
Columbia, SC 29201
(803) 765-5861

TENNESSEE
VA Regional Office
110 9th Ave S
Nashville, TN 37203
(615) 736-5251

OKLAHOMA
VA Regional Office
125 S Main St
Muskogee, OK 74401
(918) 687-2500

PENNSYLVANIA
VA Regional Office
PO Box 8079
Philadelphia, PA 19101
(215) 438-5225

PHILIPPINES
VA Regional Office
1131 Roxas Blvd
APO AP 96440
(810) 521-7521

RHODE ISLAND
VA Regional Office
380 Westminster Mall
Providence, RI 02903
(401) 273-4910

SOUTH DAKOTA
VA Regional Office
2501 W 22nd St
Sioux Falls, SD 57117
(605) 336-3496

TEXAS
VA Regional Office
6900 Almedia Rd
Houston, TX 77030
(713) 791-1378

TEXAS
VA Regional Office
1400 N Valley Mills Dr
Waco, TX 76799
(817) 772-3060

UTAH
VA Regional Office
125 S State St
Salt Lake City, UT 84147
(801) 524-5960

VERMONT
VA Regional Office
N Hartland Rd
White River Jnct, VT 05001
(802) 296-5177

VIRGINIA
VA Regional Office
210 Franklin Rd SW
Roanoke, VA 24011
(703) 857-2109

WASHINGTON
VA Regional Office
915 2nd Ave
Seattle, WA 98174
(206) 624-7200

WEST VIRGINIA
VA Regional Office
640 4th Ave
Huntington, WV 25701
(304) 529-5720

WISCONSIN
VA Regional Office
5000 W National Ave
Milwaukee, WI 53295
(414) 383-8680

WYOMING
VA Regional Office
2360 E Pershing Blvd
Cheyenne, WY 82001
(307) 778-7396

Obtain A Veteran's SSN Through The VA

You may be able to obtain a veteran's SSN from the VA if the veteran applied for benefits after April 1973. Write a letter to the VA and ask for the veteran's VA Claim number (do not ask for the veteran's SSN). Provide the veteran's name, service number or DOB. Include a check in the amount of $2.00 made payable to "Department of Veterans Affairs". If the number returned is the letter C followed by nine digits then it is the veteran's SSN. Mail your request to:

VA Records Processing Center
PO Box 5020
St. Louis, MO 63115

Federal Aviation Administration

The Federal Aviation Administration (FAA) will provide a pilot's current address if you provide the name and date of birth, SSN or a FAA pilot certificate number. If the name is unique, they can provide the information without these identifying items. The pilot's records are annotated with the name and address of the person who requested his address.

FAA Airmen Certification Branch, AVN-460
PO Box 25082   (405) 954-3261
Oklahoma City, OK 73125

Federal Courts

If the subject was involved in a federal case, the **US District Court** where the case was tried will have information such as legal name, aliases, address and SSN. If the subject has declared bankruptcy, the US Bankruptcy Court will have this same information. There is at least one US District and one US Bankruptcy Court in each state. *The Sourcebook of Federal Courts, US District and Bankruptcy,* by BRB Publications, lists the addresses and phone numbers of each court. It also describes the various procedures to obtain or review court records. Records are normally kept on file for two to five years after the case is closed. You can also call the **Federal Information Center** for the appropriate address.

Federal Information Center

The Federal Information Center will provide addresses and telephone numbers of federal agencies (executive branch, congressional offices and federal courts) throughout the United States. They will assist in providing the name of agencies that are responsible or have jurisdiction over a particular subject or area. This is an excellent resource for obtaining information or locations of any federal agency. The centralized number for all of the United States is **(800) 688-9889.**

Internal Revenue Service

The Internal Revenue Service (IRS) will forward letters for humane reasons to people in their files that they can identify with a Social Security number. Such cases include:

- Urgent or compelling nature, such as a serious illness.
- Imminent death or death of a close relative.
- A person seeking a missing relative.

A reunion or tracing a family tree does not qualify as a humane purpose. The IRS will not forward letters concerning debts. If a letter is forwarded by the IRS and is undeliverable by the post office and returned to the IRS, it will be destroyed and the sender will not be notified.

If an address can be found, the letter will be placed in an IRS envelope and the addressee will be advised that the letter is being forwarded in accordance with current IRS policy. The IRS will not divulge the recipient's current address, nor any tax information. The decision to reply is entirely up to the recipient. Check the telephone book for the nearest IRS office.

Obtain An Ex-Spouse's Social Security Number

Individuals who are divorced and cannot remember the SSN of their former spouse may request a copy of any joint income tax returns from the Internal Revenue Service. These returns will contain the SSN of the former spouse.

Library Of Congress

If you have the opportunity to visit the Library of Congress in Washington, DC, do so. There are literally millions of books and reference materials that can be of help. Of particular interest to searchers, the Library of Congress has one of the largest collections of city directories in the nation. For additional information, call **(202) 707-5000.**

Merchant Marines
(See US Coast Guard)

National Archives

The General Branch, Civil Archives Division of the National Archives, has naturalization proceedings of the District of Columbia courts, 1802-1926. These records show, for each person who petitioned for naturalization, name, age or date of birth, nationality, and whether or not citizenship was granted. The staff will search these records for information about naturalizations that occurred before September 27, 1906. The full name of the petitioner and the approximate date of naturalization must be provided.

National Personnel Records Center

The National Personnel Records Center (NPRC) is a branch of the National Archives. When a member of the armed forces separates from the service due to discharge, retirement or death, the personnel file of that veteran goes to the NPRC. There are approximately 60 million records deposited here.

In certain situations, the NPRC will forward correspondence to the last known address of a veteran. An

address is put into their military personnel records when the
veteran separates from active duty, when his reserve
commitment is completed, or if the veteran writes to NPRC
after his discharge. Correspondence is forwarded only in
the following limited situations. There is no charge except
where noted.

- Requester's VA or Social Security benefits are
  dependent on contacting the veteran.
- Veteran to be contacted will have veterans benefits
  affected.
- Veterans may have fathered illegitimate children.
- Forwarding is in the best interest of the veteran or
  next of kin e.g., estate settlement.
- A legitimate effort to collect a debt. A search fee of
  $3.50 is applicable only when the forwarding of
  correspondence is not in the veteran's interest, e.g.,
  debt collection. Make checks payable to "Treasurer
  of the United States."

The NPRC will place the letter to be forwarded in another
envelope and will add the individual's name and last known
address. In the event the letter is not delivered, it will be
returned to the NPRC and the sender will not be informed.
Mail all correspondence to:

National Personnel Records Center
9700 Page Boulevard
St. Louis, MO 63132

Acquire Information From Military Records

To obtain identifying information on a subject who was in
the military, it may be necessary to acquire it from his or her
military personnel files. The most important item of
information is the individual's date of birth. This

information may be obtained from the military files held at the NPRC. Anyone may receive the following limited information from NPRC if requested under the Freedom of Information Act:

- Rank/grade
- Name
- Service number
- Date of birth
- Dependents (including name, sex and age)
- Geographical location of duty assignments
- Source of commission (officers)
- Military/civilian education level
- Awards and decorations
- Official photograph
- Record of court-martial trials (unless classified)
- City/town, state of last known residence; date of that address
- Places of induction and separation
- Place of birth, date and location of death and place of burial of deceased veterans can also be released.

Because of the Privacy Act, the general public will not be provided with medical information, SSN or present address of any current or former living member of the military.

The information in the military records may be requested by letter (see **Appendix B**) or with a Standard Form 180 (see **Appendix C**). This form or a photocopy may be used. Additional copies of this form may be obtained from most veterans organizations, military installations or from the NPRC. For the latter, you may call any of the three telephone numbers listed below and leave a message with your name and address. A Standard Form 180 will be mailed.

Army	**(314) 538-4261**
Air Force	**(314) 538-4243**
Navy, USMC, USCG	**(314) 538-4141**

Include as much information as is known about the individual such as: name, branch of service, SSN or service number, service dates, date of birth, etc. In Section II Paragraph 1 of the SF 180, put "request all releasable information under the Freedom of Information Act" or include this statement if your request is made in a letter. No fees are charged for Freedom of Information requests, but it may take from one to six months to be processed. The NPRC receives approximately 200,000 letters and requests per month.

NOTE: In July 1973, a fire at the NPRC destroyed about 80 percent of the records for Army personnel discharged between November 1, 1912 and January 1, 1960. About 75 percent of the records for Air Force personnel with surnames from Hubbard through "Z" who were discharged between September 25, 1947 and January 1, 1964 were also destroyed. No Navy, Coast Guard or Marine Corps records were destroyed. There are currently 60 million military records at the NPRC.

Request for information from records should be mailed to:

National Personnel Records Center
9700 Page Boulevard
St. Louis, MO 63132

In addition to acquiring partial information from records under the Freedom of Information Act, the complete records may also be obtained with either the consent of the veteran or by a court order signed by a judge. For more information, see **Appendix D**.

Office Of Personnel Management

Locate Civil Service Employees

The Office of Personnel Management operates a centralized service that will locate most federal civil service employees, except those employed by the judicial and congressional offices, US Postal Service, Tennessee Valley Authority, General Accounting Office, FBI and other intelligence agencies. The only information that is permitted to be released is the name and address of the individual's employing agency, the location of his actual place of employment or the address of the agency's personnel office. The latter will provide address of work site if their policy permits.

To request a search, submit the person's name and social security number. Allow two weeks for replies to written requests. Telephone requests will only be taken for one or two names.

US Office of Personnel Management   (202) 606-2133
1900 E Street, NW
Room 7494
Washington, DC 20415

The following are the telephone numbers of the major federal agencies' personnel offices that are not included in the above search:

US Public Health Service	(301) 443-2403
Central Intelligence Agency	(703) 613-8170
Federal Bureau of Investigations	(202) 324-4164
US Postal Service	(202) 268-2000
National Oceanic and Atmospheric Administration	(800) 299-6622
Government Accounting Office	(202) 512-5811

Tennessee Valley Authority	(615) 632-2101
Senate Employees	(202) 224-3207
House of Representatives Employees	(202) 225-6514
Employees of Federal Courts	(202) 273-2777

Locate Civil Service Employees Through Local Offices

If you know which federal agency an individual works for in a particular city, you may contact that agency's local personnel office and determine the person's work place and telephone number. The same is true for individuals who work on military bases. Each military base has a civilian personnel locator. Call the base information operator for the telephone number.

Selective Service Commission

The classification records of individuals who were registered for the draft under the **Selective Service Act** and information from ledger books are available to the public. These classification records list name, date of birth, draft classification, date to report for induction and, in some cases, date of separation. Records were maintained from 1940 to 1975. These records are maintained at various federal records centers (by state and county). County records are also available in some main libraries. All requests from the **Federal Records Centers** for information, if available, must be made through:

National Headquarters　　Born before 1960 (703) 235-2555
Selective Service System　Born in/after 1960 (708) 688-6888
1550 Wilson Blvd # 601
Arlington, VA 22209-2426

Social Security Administration

The Social Security Administration (SSA) will forward some unsealed letters to people whose names are listed in their files. This will be done for certain humanitarian reasons that will be beneficial to the receiver e.g., locating missing relatives, medical needs, locating heirs to estates, assisting people with claims, etc. Letters that are accepted will be forwarded to their employers or directly to the individual if he or she is drawing Social Security benefits.

Before offering assistance, the SSA must determine that it is reasonable to assume the person to be contacted would want to receive the letter and want to reply.

The SSA will not offer to forward any correspondence unless the following conditions are met:

1. Strong compelling reasons exist, e.g.,

   a. a strong humanitarian purpose will be served (e.g., a close relative is seriously ill, is dying, or has died).
   b. a minor child is left without parental guidance.
   c. a defendant in a felony case is seeking a defense witness.
   d. a parent wishes to locate a son or daughter.
   e. consent of the missing person is needed in connection with an adoption proceeding for his/her child.

2. The missing person would want to know the contents of the letter.

3. The missing person's disappearance occurred recently enough that SSA could reasonably expect to have a usable mailing address.

4. All other possibilities for contacting the missing person have been exhausted.

Forwarding Procedures

You must submit your request in writing to the SSA, giving the following information:

1. Missing person's name and Social Security number (SSN).

2. If SSN is unknown, give date and place of birth, name of parents, name and address of last known employer and period of employment.

3. Reason for wanting to contact the person.

4. Last time seen.

5. Other contacts that have been exhausted.

Enclose your letter to be forwarded in an unsealed stamped envelope. SSA will try to find an address in their records for the missing person. If an address is found, they will forward your letter. They will tell you if they cannot forward a letter because they cannot locate a Social Security number for the missing person. The SSA cannot tell you whether:

- They found an address for the missing person.
- They were able to forward a letter to the missing person.

If Monetary Consideration Exists

A strong compelling reason may be deemed to exist if a monetary or other consideration is involved and it is reasonable to assume that the missing person does not know. For example:

- Missing person is a beneficiary of an estate.
- Insurance proceeds are due the missing person.
- An important document is being held. (SSA will not forward the document.)

The procedures are the same as above, except include a personal check, cashier's check, or money order payable to the "Social Security Administration" in the amount of $3.00 per letter.

Always ask for a receipt if you make a payment. Sometimes the clerks will write the individual's SSN on the receipt. If you are seeking someone who has changed their name, the new name may be listed on the receipt. If some new information is gathered from the receipt, you can attempt some of the computer searches in **Chapter Ten**.

In the event they cannot help you and you have prepaid a fee, the Treasury Department will mail a refund. They will state that you overpaid them or that they do not charge a fee in your case.

Mail all correspondence to:

Social Security Administration   (800) 772-1213
Office of Central Records Operations
300 N Greene Street
Baltimore, MD 21201

US Coast Guard

Locate Active Duty Coast Guard Personnel

Military Personnel Command   (202) 267-1340
Locator Service (MPC/ADM-3)   FAX (202) 267-4985
2100 Second Street, SW
Washington, DC 20593-0001
$5.20 search fee.

Locate Reserve Coast Guard Personnel

Military Personnel Command   (202) 267-0547
Locator Service (GRSM-3)   FAX (202) 267-4553
2100 Second St, SW, Room 5500
Washington, DC 20593-0001
$5.20 search fee.

Locate Retired Coast Guard Personnel

Retired Military Affairs Branch   (202) 267-2259
G-PMP-2   FAX (202) 267-4823
2100 Second St., SW
Washington, DC 20593-0001

Locate Former Coast Guard Personnel

The Coast Guard will forward letters to former members of the Coast Guard to their last known address. There is no fee for this service. Send letters to:

Military Personnel Command
Correspondence
(MPC/ADM -3)
2100 Second Street, SW
Washington, DC 20593-0001

These individuals may also be located through the VA and the National Personnel Records Center.

Locate Merchant Seamen

The US Coast Guard registers all merchant seamen and will forward a letter to the last known address of the mariner. There is no fee for this service. Place your letter in an envelope with a stamp and no return address and mail it to:

Commandant	(202) 267-0234
US Coast Guard (G-MVP-6)	FAX (202) 267-4570
2100 Second Street, SW	
Washington, DC 20593-0001	

Locate Merchant Seamen Through The VA

Merchant seamen who served in World War II (December 7, 1941 to August 15, 1945), have veteran status and you may be able to contact any of these mariners through the Department of Veterans Affairs. Many merchant seamen have served in the armed forces and have veteran status.

US Congress

If you are not getting results or answers from federal agencies or the military, write or call your United States Representative or Senator and ask for their assistance. Federal agencies and the armed forces are very responsive to inquiries from members of Congress. You can expect a quick reply to your letter, usually within two weeks.

Include all the information you can about the person you are trying to locate, why you need to contact him, what steps you have taken so far and the results of these steps.

The telephone number for the US Capitol in Washington, DC is **(202) 224-3121**. Ask the operator for the office of your Senator or Representative.

To write your Representative, the address is:

Honorable "John Doe"
United States House of Representatives
Washington, DC 20515

To write your Senator, the address is:

Honorable "John Doe"
United States Senate
Washington, DC 20510

See your local telephone book for your Congressman's name and telephone number. It will help if you call the local office first and talk to the administrative assistant about the difficulties you are encountering.

US Government Printing Office

This office sells numerous books published by the government, many of which are valuable to searchers. Some of these books include:

US Government Organization Manual - this lists the address, telephone number and description of each federal agency and office.

Directory Of US Government Depository Libraries - this lists libraries throughout the country that have federal publications.

Where To Write For Vital Records - this provides details on how to obtain birth, death, marriage and divorce records from each state. For more information, contact:

Superintendent Of Documents   (202) 512-1800
US Government Printing Office
Washington, DC 20402

US Marshal

If your subject may be wanted by federal authorities, contact the local US Marshal. They should be listed in your local telephone directory.

US Postal Service

For many years, anyone could obtain an individual's new address from the US Post Office under the FOIA, if the individual had submitted a change of address card. This practice was discontinued as of April 1994. However, the US Postal Change of Address file is still available to credit bureaus, information providers and many computer databases (see **Chapter Ten** for details).

You may still be able to obtain an individual's new address by mailing a letter to the person's last known address and writing "ADDRESS CORRECTION REQUESTED" on the lower edge of the envelope or below the return address. The post office will place a label showing the new address and return your letter to you. You may write "DO NOT FORWARD" and the letter will be returned with the individual's new address. Change of address information is retained by the post office for eighteen months, but they will forward letters for only 12 months. There is a fee of thirty-five cents for this service. You might want to use this method when forwarding letters through the armed forces world-wide locators, base locators, alumni associations and the Social Security Administration. It is possible to find the person's current address in this manner.

By writing the postmaster (especially in small towns) where the person once lived, you may obtain some useful information and assistance. Many small town postmasters have held their jobs for 30 to 40 years and know the location or relatives of numerous people who once lived there.

The National ZIP Code Directory

The US Postal Service publishes the *National ZIP Code Directory* which lists all cities in the US with a post office, their ZIP codes, and the county where the city is located. Streets are listed for larger cities. This book is available for purchase or use in all US Post Offices. It is also available in most libraries.

If you request information from the federal government and the armed forces under the Freedom of Information Act, **Appendix B** is an example of the format you should use.

Chapter Six

Where To Obtain Information And Assistance From State Governments

It is possible to obtain identifying information and addresses of individuals through birth, marriage and divorce records, motor vehicle registration, driver license records and professional regulating agencies of the various states.

State Parent Locator Service

The federal government will make a computer search of IRS, VA and the Social Security Administration files for anyone who has a child support court order against them. If the name is listed, the address and SSN of the individual will be provided.

To obtain this service, all requests must be made to the appropriate state parent locator service in the child support enforcement bureau. Check the local telephone book for address and telephone number or call the state information number listed later in this chapter.

Obtain Identifying Information Through Birth, Marriage And Divorce Records

Vital records consists of birth and death certificates, marriage licenses, divorce and annulment decrees. Each Vital Records office has different fee and information requirements according to the laws of their state/area. Some states will release these records to family members only. If you are not sure if an individual is deceased, see **Chapter Nine**.

Note: In many states, certain vital records are only available from the county where they were issued.

Provide as much of the following information as possible in order to obtain a copy of the birth or death certificate:

- Full name of person whose record is being requested
- Sex and race
- Date of birth and date of death (if applicable)
- Place of birth or death (city or town, county and state; and name of hospital, if any)
- Parents' names, including maiden name of mother
- Purpose for which copy is needed
- Relationship to person whose record is being requested

Provide as much of the following information as possible in order to obtain a copy of the marriage license:

- Full names of bride and groom (including nicknames)
- Residence addresses at time of marriage
- Ages at time of marriage (or dates of birth)
- Month, day and year of marriage

- Place of marriage (city or town, county and state)
- Purpose for which copy is needed
- Relationship to person whose record is being requested

Provide as much of the following information as possible in order to obtain a copy of the divorce or annulment decree:

- Full names of husband and wife (including nicknames)
- Present residence address
- Former addresses (as in court records)
- Ages at time of divorce (or dates of birth)
- Date of divorce or annulment
- Place of divorce or annulment
- Type of final decree
- Purpose for which copy is needed
- Relationship to person whose record is being requested

Below are the addresses of the offices where copies of birth, death, marriage, divorce and annulment records can be obtained.

The charges for services vary by state. Please check with the state for fees and services available.

ALABAMA
Center for Health Statistics
Vital Records Division
PO Box 5625
Montgomery, AL 36103
(334) 613-5418
• Divorce decrees by county

ALASKA
Dept of Health & Social Srvcs
Bureau of Vital Statistics
PO Box 110675
Juneau, AK 99811
(907) 465-3392

ARIZONA
Dept of Health Services
Vital Records Section
PO Box 3887
Phoenix, AZ 85030
(602) 255-3260
• Divorce decrees by county

ARKANSAS
Arkansas Dept of Health
Division of Vital Records
4815 W Markham Street
Little Rock, AR 72205
(501) 661-2134
• Divorce decrees by county

CALIFORNIA
Office of the State Registrar
PO Box 730241
Al
Sacramento, CA 95814
(916) 445-2684
• Divorce decrees by county

COLORADO
Colorado Dept of Health
Vital Records Section -HSVR-

4300 Cherry Creek Dr, South
Denver, CO 80222
(303) 756-4464
• Divorce/Marriage by county

CONNECTICUT
Dept of Health Services
Vital Records Section
150 Washington Street
Hartford, CT 06106
(203) 566-1124
• Divorce decrees by county

DELAWARE
Dept of Public Health
Office of Vital Statistics
PO Box 637
Dover, DE 19903
(302) 739-4721
• Divorce decrees by county

DISTRICT OF COLUMBIA
Dept of Health
Vital Records Branch
613 G St, NW, 9th Floor
Washington, DC 20001
(202) 727-9281 (*birth/death*)

DISTRICT OF COLUMBIA
Superior Court House
500 Indiana Ave, NW
Washington, DC 20001
Marriage - (202) 879-4850
Divorce - (202) 879-1410

FLORIDA

Dept of Health & Rehab Svcs
Office of Vital Statistics
PO Box 210
Jacksonville, FL 32231
(904) 359-6900

GEORGIA

Georgia Dept of Hmn Rscs
Vital Records Unit
47 Trinity Ave SW Rm 217H
Atlanta, GA 30334
(404) 656-7456
• Divorce decrees by county

HAWAII

State Dept of Health
Vital Records Section
PO Box 3378
Honolulu, HI 96801
(808) 586-4539

IDAHO

State Dept of Health
Center for Vital Statistics
450 West State Street
State House Mail
Boise, ID 83720-9990
(208) 334-5988

ILLINOIS

State Dept of Public Health
Division of Vital Records
605 West Jefferson Street
Springfield, IL 62702
(217) 782-6553
• Divorce/Marriage by county

INDIANA

State Dept of Health
Vital Records Section
PO Box 1964
Indianapolis, IN 46206
(317) 633-0701
• Divorce decrees by county

IOWA

Iowa Dept of Public Health
Vital Records Section
Lucas Office Building
321 East 12th St, 4th Floor
Des Moines, IA 50319-0075
(515) 281-4944
• Divorce decrees by county

KANSAS

Kansas State Dept of Health
  and Environment
Office of Vital Statistics
900 SW Jackson Street
Landon State Office Bldg
Topeka, KS 66612
(913) 296-1400

KENTUCKY
Dept for Human Services
Vital Statistics
275 East Main Street
Frankfort, KY 40621
(502) 564-4212

LOUISIANA
Dept of Vital Records
PO Box 60630
New Orleans, LA 70160
(504) 568-4980
• Divorce/Marriage by county

MAINE
Maine Dept of Human Srvcs
Vital Records
State House Station 11
Augusta, ME 04333
(207) 287-3181

MARYLAND
Dept of Health
Division of Vital Records
PO Box 68760
Baltimore, MD 21215
(410) 764-3038

MASSACHUSETTS
Registry Vital Records/Stats
150 Tremont St, Room B-3
Boston, MA 02111
(617) 727-0110
• Divorce decrees by county

MICHIGAN
Michigan Dept of Health
Office of the State Registrar
PO Box 30195
Lansing, MI 48909
(517) 335-8656

MINNESOTA
Minnesota Dept of Health
Section of Vital Records
717 Delaware Street, SE
Minneapolis, MN 55414
(612) 623-5120
• Divorce/Marriage by county

MISSISSIPPI
State Dept of Health
Vital Records
PO Box 1700
Jackson, MS 39215
(601) 960-7981

MISSOURI
Missouri Dept of Health
Bureau of Vital Records
PO Box 570
Jefferson City, MO 65102
(314) 751-6387
• Divorce/Marriage by county

MONTANA
Montana Dept of Health
Vital Records
1400 Broadway
Cogswell Bldg, Rm C118
Helena, MT 56920
(406) 444-4228
• Divorce/Marriage by county

NEBRASKA
State Dept of Health
Bureau of Vital Statistics
PO Box 95007
Lincoln, NE 68509-5007
(402) 471-2871

NEVADA
Dept of Health
Office of Vital Statistics
505 East King Street
Carson City, NV 89710
(702) 687-4481
• Divorce/Marriage by county

NEW HAMPSHIRE
Dept of Health
Bureau of Vital Records
6 Hazen Drive
Concord, NH 03301
(603) 271-4650

NEW JERSEY
State Dept of Health
Vital Statistics
CN 370
Trenton, NJ 08625
(609) 292-4087

NEW MEXICO
Dept of Health
Bureau of Vital Records
PO Box 26110
Santa Fe, NM 87502
(505) 827-2338
• Divorce/Marriage by county

NEW YORK
State Dept of Health
Vital Records Section
Empire State Plaza
Corning Tower Building
Albany, NY 12237
(518) 474-3038

NEW YORK CITY
Dept of Health
Bureau of Vital Records
PO Box 3776
Church Street Station
New York, NY 10007
(212) 788-4506
• Death/Marriage-Borough records
• Divorce-local courts

NORTH CAROLINA
Dept of Environment, Health,
  and Natural Resources
Vital Records Section
PO Box 29537
Raleigh, NC 27626
(919) 733-3526

NORTH DAKOTA
State Dept of Health
Vital Records
600 East Blvd Ave, 1st Floor
Bismarck, ND 58505
(701) 224-2360
• Divorce decrees by county

OHIO
Ohio Dept of Health
Bureau of Vital Statistics
PO Box 118
Columbus, OH 43266-0118
(614) 466-2531
• Divorce/Marriage by county

OKLAHOMA
State Dept of Health
Vital Records Section
PO Box 53551
Oklahoma City, OK 73152
(405) 271-4040
• Divorce/Marriage by county

OREGON
Oregon Health Division
Vital Records
PO Box 14050
Portland, OR 97214
(503) 731-4095

PENNSYLVANIA
Division of Vital Records
State Dept of Health
PO Box 1528
New Castle, PA 16103
(412) 656-3100
• Divorce/Marriage by county

RHODE ISLAND
State Dept of Health
Capitol Hill, Cannon Building
Room 101
Providence, RI 02908
(401) 277-2812
• Divorce decrees by county

SOUTH CAROLINA
South Carolina DHEC
Office of Vital Records
2600 Bull Street
Columbia, SC 29201
(803) 734-4830

SOUTH DAKOTA
State Dept of Health
Vital Records
445 E. Capitol
Pierre, SD 57501
(605) 773-4961

TENNESSEE
Tennessee Dept of Health
Vital Records
Cordell Hull Bldg, C3-324
Nashville, TN 37247-0350
(615) 741-1763

TEXAS
Texas Dept of Health
Bureau of Vital Statistics
1100 West 49th Street
Austin, TX 78756
(512) 458-7111

UTAH
State Dept of Health
Bureau of Vital Records
PO Box 16700
Salt Lake City, UT 84116
(801) 538-6380

VERMONT
Vermont Dept of Health
Vital Records Section
PO Box 70
Burlington, VT 05402
(802) 863-7275

VIRGINIA
State Health Dept
Division of Vital Records
PO Box 1000
Richmond, VA 23208
(804) 786-6228

WASHINGTON
Dept of Health
Vital Records
PO Box 9709
Olympia, WA 98507
(206) 753-5842

WEST VIRGINIA
Bureau of Public Health
Vital Records
State Capitol Complex
Building 3, Room 516
Charleston, WV 25305
(304) 558-2931

WISCONSIN
Center of Health Statistics
Vital Records
PO Box 309
Madison, WI 53701
(608) 266-1372

WYOMING
Dept of Health
Vital Records Services
Hathaway Building
Cheyenne, WY 82002
(307) 777-7591

OVERSEAS BIRTHS
Authentication Office
21st St & Virginia Ave NW
Washington, DC 20025

OVERSEAS BIRTHS
Passport Services
State Department
Washington, DC 20524

Obtain Information Through State Driver License Offices

At present, sixteen states usually use the **Social Security number** (SSN) as the driver license number: Arizona, Arkansas, District of Columbia, Georgia, Hawaii, Iowa, Kansas, Kentucky, Massachusetts, Missouri, Mississippi, Montana, North Dakota, Oklahoma, South Dakota and Virginia. Some other states, including Florida and Ohio, make the **SSN** part of the driver's record. Obtaining a copy of the driving record in most of these states will provide the individual's SSN.

Nevada derives driver license (DL) numbers from the driver's **SSN** using a mathematical formula. If you know that formula, you can reverse the process and obtain the SSN from the DL number.

Forty-six states and the District of Columbia will provide the current reported address of individuals who have a driver license or identification card in their respective states. Four states (California, Georgia, Massachusetts and Virginia) will not provide an address, but will forward letters to the individual. There are computer searches available that will provide the current, reported address from state driver license files.

Contact each state office for information and fee requirements.

ALABAMA
DPS, Driver License Division
PO Box 1471
Montgomery, AL 36102
(334) 242-4400

ALASKA
DMV, Drivers Records
PO Box 20020
Juneau, AK 99802
(907) 465-4335

ARIZONA
Motor Vehicle Division
Record Services Section
Box 2100, Mail Drop 504M
Phoenix, AZ 85001
(602) 255-7865

ARKANSAS
Dept of Driver Services
Driver Records Division
PO Box 1272, Rm 127
Little Rock, AR 72203
(501) 682-7207

CALIFORNIA
Dept of Motor Vehicles
Info Request Counter
Box 944231 Mail Sta C198
Sacramento, CA 94244
(916) 657-8098

COLORADO
Motor Vehicle Division
Traffic Records
104 W 6th Ave, Rm 103
Denver, CO 80204
(303) 623-9463

CONNECTICUT
Dept of Motor Vehicles
Copy Records Section
60 State St Room 305
Wethersfield, CT 06109
(203) 566-7740

DELAWARE
Division of Motor Vehicles
Driver Services
PO Box 698
Dover, DE 19903
(302) 739-4343

DISTRICT OF COLUMBIA
Dept of Motor Vehicles
Driver Records Division
301 "C" St NW, Rm 1157
Washington, DC 20001
(202) 727-6761

FLORIDA
Dept of Public Safety
Division of Drivers Licenses
2900 Apalachee Pkwy Rm B239
Tallahassee, FL 32399
(904) 487-2369

GEORGIA
Dept of Motor Vehicles
Drivers License Section
MVR Unit, PO Box 1456
Atlanta, GA 30371
(404) 624-7487

HAWAII
Traffic Violations Bureau
Abstract Section
1111 Alakea Street
Honolulu, HI 96813
(808) 548-5735

IDAHO
Idaho Transportation Dept
Drivers Services
PO Box 34
Boise, ID 83701
(208) 334-8736

ILLINOIS
Driver Analysis Section
Drivers Services Dept
2701 S Dirksen Pkwy
Springfield, IL 62723
(217) 782-2720

INDIANA
Bureau of Motor Vehicles
Driver Records
Rm N405, IN Gov Cen, N
Indianapolis, IN 46204
(317) 232-2894

IOWA
Dept of Transportation
Driver Service Records Sec
PO Box 9204
Des Moines, IA 50306
(515) 237-3070

KANSAS
Department of Revenue
Driver Control Bureau
PO Box 12021
Topeka, KS 66612
(913) 296-3671

KENTUCKY
Division of Drivers Licensing
MVRS-State Office Building
501 High Street, 2nd Floor
Frankfort, KY 40622
(502) 564-4711

LOUISIANA
Dept of Public Safety
 and Corrections
Office of Motor Vehicles
PO Box 64886
Baton Rouge, LA 70896
(504) 925-6009

MAINE
Bureau of Motor Vehicles
Driver License & Control
State House Station 29
Augusta, ME 04333
(207) 287-2576

MARYLAND
Motor of Motor Vehicles
Motor Vehicle Admin
6601 Richie Hwy, NE
 Counter 212
Glen Burnie, MD 21062
(410) 787-7705

MASSACHUSETTS
Registrar of Motor Vehicles
1135 Tremont St
Boston, MA 02120
(617) 351-9834

MICHIGAN
Dept of State Police
Commercial Look-up Unit
7064 Crowner Dr
Lansing, MI 48918
(517) 322-1624

MINNESOTA
Driver and Vehicle Services-
Investigation Unit
Record Request
395 John Ireland Blvd Rm 108
St. Paul, MN 55155
(612) 296-2023

MISSISSIPPI
Dept of Public Safety
Driver Records
PO Box 958
Jackson, MS 39205
(601) 987-1274

MISSOURI
Dept of Revenue
Driver License Bureau
PO Box 200
Jefferson City, MO 65105
(314) 751-4600

MONTANA
Motor Vehicle Division
Drivers' Services
PO Box 201419
Helena, MT 59620
(406) 444-4590

NEBRASKA
Dept of Motor Vehicles
Driver Records
PO Box 94789
Lincoln, NE 68509
(402) 471-4343

NEVADA
Dept. of Motor Vehicles
and Public Safety
555 Wright Way
Carson City, NV 89711
(702) 687-5505

NEW HAMPSHIRE
Dept of Motor Vehicles
Driving Records
10 Hazen Dr
Concord, NH 03305
(603) 271-2322

NEW JERSEY
Motor Vehicle Services
Drivers Abstract Section
CN 142
Trenton, NJ 08666
(609) 633-8255

NEW MEXICO
Dept of Motor Vehicles
Driver Services Bureau
PO Box 1028
Santa Fe, NM 87504
(505) 827-2241

NEW YORK
Dept. of Motor Vehicles
Div of Data Prep & Control
Rm 430, Empire St Plaza
Albany, NY 12228
(518) 474-2381

NORTH CAROLINA
Dept of Motor Vehicles
Drivers License Section
1100 New Bern Ave
Raleigh, NC 27697
(919) 733-4241

NORTH DAKOTA
Dept of Transportation
Driver License & Traffic
  Safety Division
608 E Boulevard Ave
Bismarck, ND 58505
(701) 224-2603

OHIO
Dept of Motor Vehicles
Bureau of Motor Vehicles
4300 Kimberly Pkwy
Columbus, OH 43232
(614) 752-7600

OKLAHOMA
Dept of Public Safety
Drivers Record Services
PO Box 11415
Oklahoma City, OK 73136
(405) 425-2026

OREGON
Dept of Motor Vehicles
1905 Lana Ave NE
Salem, OR 97314
(503) 945-5000

PENNSYLVANIA
Dept of Transportation
Information Sales Unit
PO Box 68691
Harrisburg, PA 17106
(717) 787-3130

RHODE ISLAND
Driving Records Clerk
Operator Control
345 Harris Ave
Providence, RI 02909
(401) 277-2994

SOUTH CAROLINA
Dept of Public Safety
Driver Records Section
PO Box 1498
Columbia, SC 29216
(803) 251-2940

SOUTH DAKOTA
Div of Commerce & Reg
Drivers License Program
118 W Capitol
Pierre, SD 57501
(605) 773-3191

TENNESSEE
Dept of Safety, Financial
  Responsibility Section
Driving License & Driving
  Records
1150 Foster Ave
Nashville, TN 37249
(615) 741-3954

UTAH
Dept of Public Safety
Drivers License &
  Driving Records Section
PO Box 30560
Salt Lake City, UT 84119
(801) 965-4430

VIRGINIA
Dept of Motor Vehicles
Motorist Info Administration
PO Box 27412
Richmond, VA 23269
(804) 367-0538

WEST VIRGINIA
Division of Motor Vehicles
Safety & Enforcement
1900 Kanawha Blvd
Charleston, WV 25317
(304) 558-0238

WYOMING
Wyoming Dept of Trans
Driver Services
PO Box 1708
Cheyenne, WY 82003
(307) 777-4802

TEXAS
License Issuance &
  Driver Records
Driver Records Section
PO Box 15999
Austin, TX 78761
(512) 465-2032

VERMONT
Dept of Motor Vehicles
Driver Improvement Info
120 State St
Montpelier, VT 05603
(802) 828-2050

WASHINGTON
Dept of Licensing
Drivers Responsibility Div
PO Box 9030
Olympia, WA 98507
(206) 753-6976

WISCONSIN
Dept of Motor Vehicles
License Record Section
PO Box 7918
Madison, WI 53707
(608) 264-7060

Obtain Addresses Through State Motor Vehicle Registration Offices

Contact the appropriate state office to obtain someone's address from an automobile license, vehicle plate number, registration or title. This service usually requires a fee. Check with the state office for further information.

ALABAMA
Motor Vehicle Division
Title & Registration Section
PO Box 327640
Montgomery, AL 36132
(334) 242-9000

ALASKA
Dept. of Motor Vehicles
ATTN: Research
2150 E Dowling Rd
Anchorage, AK 99507
(907) 563-5589

ARIZONA
Motor Vehicle Division
Records Services Section
Box 2100, Mail Drop 504M
Phoenix, AZ 85001
(602) 255-7865

ARKANSAS
Office of Motor Vehicles
IRP Unit
PO Box 1272, Room 106
Little Rock, AR 72203
(501) 682-3333

CALIFORNIA
Dept of Motor Vehicles
Consulting Room
Box 944247, Mail Sta C198
Sacramento, CA 94244
(916) 657-8098

COLORADO
Dept of Motor Vehicles
Vehicle Records Section
140 W 6th Avenue
Denver, CO 80204
(303) 623-9463

CONNECTICUT
Dept of Motor Vehicles
Copy Record Unit
60 State St, Branch Ops
Wethersfield, CT 06109
(203) 566-3090

DELAWARE
Division of Motor Vehicles
ATTN: Correspondence Sec
PO Box 698
Dover, DE 19903
(302) 739-3147

DISTRICT OF COLUMBIA
Dept of Motor Vehicles
Vehicle Control Division
301 "C" St NW, Rm 1063
Washington, DC 20001
(202) 727-4768

FLORIDA
Division of Motor Vehicles
Information Research Section
Neil Kirkman Bldg Room A126
Tallahassee, FL 32399
(904) 488-5665

GEORGIA
Dept of Revenue Research
270 Washington St SW
  Room 105
Atlanta, GA 30334
(404) 656-4156

HAWAII
Restricted Access
Not available to the public

IDAHO
Idaho Transportation Dept
Titles/Dealers Ops Section
PO Box 7129
Boise, ID 83707
(208) 334-8663

ILLINOIS
Vehicle Services Dept
Record Inquiry
408 Howlett Building
Springfield, IL 62756
(217) 782-6992

INDIANA
Bureau of Motor Vehicles
Vehicle Records
100 N Senate Ave, Rm N405
Indianapolis, IN 46204
(317) 232-2795

IOWA
Dept of Transportation
Office of Vehicle Reg
PO Box 9204
Des Moines, IA 50306
(515) 237-3077

KANSAS
Division of Vehicles
Title and Registration Bureau
915 Harrison
Topeka, KS 66616
(913) 296-3621

KENTUCKY
Dept of Motor Vehicles
Div of Motor Vehicle Licensing
State Office Bldg, 3rd Floor
Frankfort, KY 40622
(502) 564-2737/4076

LOUISIANA
Dept of Public Safety
and Corrections
Office of Motor Vehicles
PO Box 64884
Baton Rouge, LA 70896
(504) 925-6146

MAINE
Dept of Motor Vehicles
Registration Section
State House Station 29
Augusta, ME 04333
(207) 287-3556

MARYLAND
Dept of Motor Vehicles
Vehicle Reg Division
6601 Richie Hwy, NE
Room 206
Glen Burnie, MD 21062
(410) 768-7250

MASSACHUSETTS
Registry of Motor Vehicles
Customer Assistance-
Mail Listing Dept.
1135 Tremont St
Boston, MA 02120
(617) 351-4400

MICHIGAN
Dept of State Police
Commercial Look-Up Unit
7064 Crowner Dr
Lansing, MI 48919
(517) 322-1624

MINNESOTA
Driver and Vehicle Services
Records Dept
395 John Ireland Blvd, Rm 214
St Paul, MN 55155
(612) 296-6911

MISSISSIPPI
State Tax Comm
Registration Dept
PO Box 1140
Jackson, MS 39215
(601) 359-1248

MISSOURI
Dept of Motor Vehicles
Motor Vehicle Bureau
PO Box 100
Jefferson City MO 65105
(314) 751-4509

MONTANA
Dept of Justice
Title & Registration Bureau
925 Main St
Deer Lodge, MT 59722
(406) 846-1423

NEBRASKA
Dept of Motor Vehicles
Titles & Registration Sec
PO Box 94789
Lincoln, NE 68509
(402) 471-3910

NEVADA
Dept. of Motor Vehicles and
Public Safety
Motor Vehicle Record Sec
555 Wright Way
Carson City, NV 89711
(702) 687-5505

NEW HAMPSHIRE
Dept of Public Safety
Bureau of Title Registration
10 Hazen Drive
Concord, NH 03305
(603) 271-3111

NEW JERSEY
Motor Vehicle Services
Certified Info Unit
CN 146
Trenton, NJ 08666
(609) 588-2424

NEW MEXICO
Dept of Motor Vehicles
Vehicle Services Bureau
PO Box 1028
Santa Fe, NM 87504
(505) 827-2220

NEW YORK
Div of Data Prep & Control
Empire State Plaza
Swan St Bldg, Room 430
Albany, NY 12228
(518) 474-0642

NORTH CAROLINA
Dept of Motor Vehicles
Vehicle Registration Sec
1100 New Bern Ave
Raleigh, NC 27697
(919) 733-3025

NORTH DAKOTA
Dept of Transportation
Records Sec/Motor Veh Div
608 E Boulevard Ave
Bismarck, ND 58505
(701) 224-2725

OHIO
Bureau of Motor Vehicles
Motor Vehicle Records
4300 Kimberly Parkway
Columbus, OH 43232
(614) 752-7634

OKLAHOMA
Oklahoma Tax Comm
Motor Vehicle Division
Research
2501 N Lincoln Blvd
Oklahoma City, OK 73194
(405) 521-3221

OREGON
Driver & Motor Vehicle Ser
Customer Assistance
1905 Lana Ave NE
Salem, OR 97314
(503) 945-5000

PENNSYLVANIA
Dept of Transportation
Information Sales Unit
PO Box 68691
Harrisburg, PA 17106
(717) 787-3130

RHODE ISLAND
Registry of Motor Vehicles
c/o Registration Files
Two Capital Hill
Providence, RI 02903
(401) 277-2064

SOUTH CAROLINA
Dept of Motor Vehicles
Titles and Reg Records Sec
PO Box 1498
Columbia, SC 29216
(803) 251-2960

SOUTH DAKOTA
Div of Motor Vehicles
Information Section
118 W Capital Ave
Pierre, SD 57501
(605) 773-3541

TENNESSEE
Dept of Motor Vehicles
Titling & Registration Div
1283 Murfreesboro Road
  Suite 100
Nashville, TN 37243
(615) 741-3101

TEXAS
Dept of Transportation
Production Data Control
40th St and Jackson
Austin, TX 78779
(512) 465-7611

UTAH
State Tax Commission
Motor Vehicle Records Sec
1095 Motor Ave
Salt Lake City, UT 84116
(801) 538-8300

VERMONT
Dept of Motor Vehicles
Registr'tn & License Info/Rec
120 State St
Montpelier, VT 05603
(802) 828-2000

VIRGINIA
Management Info Admin
Vehicle Research Section
PO Box 27412
Richmond, VA 23269
(804) 367-6729

WASHINGTON
Dept of Licensing
Vehicle Services
PO Box 9030
Olympia, WA 98507
(206) 753-6990

WEST VIRGINIA
Division of Motor Vehicles
Titles and Registration Div
1608 Washington Street E
Charleston, WV 25317
(304) 558-0282

WISCONSIN
Dept of Transportation
Vehicle Records Section
PO Box 7911
Madison, WI 53707
(608) 266-3666

WYOMING
Dept of Transportation
Motor Vehicle Lic & Titles
PO Box 1708
Cheyenne, WY 82003
(307) 777-4717

Locate People In State Prisons

Each state has a prison system. To determine if your subject is or has been in a state prison, contact the State Prison Locators listed below. These locators are usually operated by the State Department of Corrections or Prisons. You may also be able to find out if your subject was ever employed by a state prison.

If the individual may be in a federal prison, telephone the **US federal prison locator** at **(202) 307-3126**. To determine if a former military member is or has been imprisoned in the **US Disciplinary Barracks** (military prison) at **Ft. Leavenworth**, Kansas, call **(913) 684-4629**.

Most prison locators keep records of former inmates for up to ten years. Surname searches may be completed without date of birth or Social Security number. Aliases may be available. The amount of information each locator will give you about the individual varies by state. The telephone numbers for the State Prison Locators are as follows:

Alabama (334) 242-9400	**Alaska** (907) 465-3376
Arizona (602) 542-5586	**Arkansas** (501) 247-1800
California (916) 445-6713	**Colorado** (719) 579-9580
Connecticut (203) 566-5710	**Delaware** (302) 739-5601
Florida (904) 488-2533	**Georgia** (404) 651-6800
Hawaii (808) 847-4491	**Idaho** (208) 334-2318
Illinois (217) 522-2666 ext.6489	**Indiana** (317) 232-5715
Iowa (515) 281-4816	**Kansas** (913) 296-7220
Kentucky (502) 564-2433	**Louisiana** (504) 655-4411
Maine (207) 354-2535	**Maryland** (410) 764-4100
Massachusetts (617) 727-7232	**Michigan** (517) 335-1426
Minnesota (612) 642-0322	**Mississippi** (601) 745-6611
Missouri (314) 751-8488	**Montana** (406) 444-3930

Nebraska (402) 471-2654	**Nevada** (702) 887-3285
New Hampshire (603) 271-1823	**New Jersey** (609) 292-0328
New Mexico (505) 827-8200	**New York** (518) 457-0034
North Carolina (919) 733-3965	**North Dakota** (328) 221-6100
Ohio (614) 752-1159	**Oklahoma** (405) 425-2624
Oregon (503) 373-1595	**Pennsylvania** (717) 737-6538
Rhode Island (401) 464-3000	**South Carolina** (803) 896-8500
South Dakota (605) 367-5190	**Tennessee** (615) 741-2733
Texas (409) 295-6371	**Utah** (801) 265-5571
Vermont (802) 241-2305	**Virginia** (804) 674-3000
Washington (360) 753-1573	**West Virginia** (304) 558-2036
Wisconsin (608) 266-2097	**Wyoming** (307) 328-1441

Locate People Through State Licensing Agencies

All states license or register trades and professions. Those that are regulated vary by state. Many cities and counties also have some licensing requirements. The following are examples of some trades and professions that are regulated. If the subject is a member of any of these occupations, contact the appropriate state, city or county licensing or regulating agency. Most agencies consider the address of these individuals to be public information, so it may be possible to obtain a former or current address. A list of state information offices is at the end of this chapter. Call for telephone numbers of the appropriate agency.

Accountants
Acupuncture
Aircraft Mechanics
Airports
Alarm Installers
Alcohol Sales
Appraisers
Architects
Athletic Announcers
Attorneys
Auctioneers
Audiologist
Auto Adjuster
Auto Appraiser
Auto Inspectors
Auto Wreckers
Bankers
Barbers
Beauticians

Builders/Carpenters
Building Contractors
Building Wreckers
Butchers
Carpet Cleaners
Certified Public
 Accountants
Check Cashing Service
Child Care/Daycare
 Centers
Chiropractors
Consumer Collection
 Agencies
Cosmetologist
Cosmetology Instructor
Counselors
Credit Unions
Debt Adjusters
Dentists/Hygienists

Detectives
Dietitians
Driving Instructors
Electricians
Embalmer
Engineers
Explosives
Food Processing
Fuel Storage
Fuel Transportation
Funeral Director
Furniture Manufacturing
Gambling
Garment Cleaners
Geologists
Hairdresser
Health Care Professionals
Hearing Aid Dealer
Heating/Air Conditioning
  Technicians
Homeopath
Hypertrichologist
Hypnotherapist
Insurance Agents
Insurance Brokers
Insurance Companies
Insurance Consultants
Insurance Investigators
Interior Designers
Investment Advisers
Laboratories
Landscape Architecture
Licensed Nurse Midwife
Licensed Practical Nurse
Liquor Licensees

Locksmiths
Lottery Control Board
Manicurist
Marriage and Family
  Therapist
Massage Therapist
Mattress Rebuilders
Meat Packers
Meat Storage
Mechanics
Medical Technicians
Mining
Money Orders/Travelers
  Checks Services
Naturopath
Notary Publics
Nursing Home
  Administrators
Nursing Homes
Occupational Therapists
Ocularists
Oil Drilling
Opticians
Optometrists
Osteopathic Physician/
  Surgeon
Painters
Pawnbrokers
Pest Controllers/
  Exterminators
Pesticide Applicators
Pet Groomers
Pharmacists
Physical Therapists
Physicians

Physician Assistants
Pilots
Plumbers
Podiatrists
Private Investigators
Private Schools
Process Servers
Psychiatrists
Psychologists
Public Transportation
(Taxis, etc.)
Public Utilities
Radiological
Technologists
Real Estate Agents and
Brokers
Registered Nurses
Respiratory Care
Practitioners
Restaurants
Savings and Loan
Companies

Schools
Scrap Dealers
Security Guards
Service Stations
Social Workers
Stock Brokers
Surveyors
Taxi Owners/Operators
Teachers
Therapists
Timbering
Trade Schools
Veterinarians
Waste Disposal
Waste Removal
Waste Storage
Water Taxis
Water Well Drillers
Weights and Measures
X-Ray Technicians

State Assistance Numbers

Call the appropriate number below to find out addresses and
telephone numbers for state agencies, offices and activities
not listed in this book which might be additional sources of
assistance or information. Examples of these are state
libraries, state archives, state National Guard headquarters
(Adjutants General offices) state military archives and
museums, state historical offices, state genealogical
societies, state hunting and fishing license offices, state
regulating offices, state parent locators, state child support

offices,   state professional regulatory boards, state tax offices, state civil service personnel offices (locators) and state government officials, etc.

Alabama
(334) 242-8000

Alaska
(907) 465-2111

Arizona
(602) 542-4900

Arkansas
(501) 682-3000

California
North (916) 322-9900

California
South (213) 620-3030

Colorado
(303) 866-5000

Connecticut
(203) 566-2211

Delaware
Kent (302) 739-4000

Delaware
NewCsl (302) 577-2011

Delaware
Sussex (302) 856-5011

Florida
(904) 488-1234

Georgia
(404) 656-2000

Hawaii
(800) 468-4644

Idaho
(208) 334-2411

Illinois
(217) 782-2000

Indiana
(317) 232-1000

Iowa
(515) 281-5011

Kansas
(913) 296-0111

Kentucky
(502) 564-3130

Louisiana
(504) 342-6600

Maine
(207) 582-9500

Maryland	**Massachusetts**
no number listed	(617) 727-7030
Michigan	**Minnesota**
(517) 373-1837	(612) 296-6013
Mississippi	**Missouri**
(601) 359-1000	(314) 751-2000
Montana	**Nebraska**
(406) 444-2511	(402) 471-2311
Nevada	**New Hampshire**
(702) 687-5000	(603) 271-1110
New Jersey	**New Mexico**
(609) 292-2121	(505) 827-4011
New York	**North Carolina**
(518) 474-2121	(919) 733-1110
North Dakota	**Ohio**
(701) 328-2000	(614) 466-2000
Oklahoma	**Oregon**
(405) 521-2011	no number listed
Pennsylvania	**Rhode Island**
(717) 787-2121	(401) 277-2000
South Carolina	**South Dakota**
(803) 734-1000	(605) 773-3011
Tennessee	**Texas**
(615) 741-3011	(512) 463-4630

Utah
(801) 538-3000

Vermont
(802) 828-1110

Virginia
(804) 786-0000

Washington
(360) 753-5000

West Virginia
(304) 558-3456

Wisconsin
(608) 266-2211

Wyoming
(307) 777-5910

Chapter Seven

Where To Obtain Information And Assistance From City And County Governments

Many city and county government offices can offer valuable assistance and identifying information.

Libraries

City and county public libraries have a wealth of information for searchers. The same may be true of college, private and other specialized libraries. They are resources that should be utilized either in person, by letter, telephone or FAX. Visit your local library and explain what you are doing to the librarian. You will definitely get a lot of valuable assistance. If you are able to actually go to libraries located in cities where your subject once lived, you will be more likely to obtain pertinent information.

Many libraries take part in the **On-Line Computer Library Center** and the **Interlibrary-Loan** programs. The On-Line Computer Library Center program can determine which libraries have the reference materials needed for your search. If are not able to go to each library, the Interlibrary

Loan program allows the books or materials needed to be sent to a library closer to you. Ask your librarian for details and procedures.

The following books and resources have proven to be of immense value to searchers. They have been divided into the categories of **General Reference**, **Search Related** and **Databases and Microfilm Information**.

General Reference

All in One Directory by Gebby Press - contains addresses, telephone numbers and FAX numbers of daily and weekly newspapers, radio and television stations, business, trade, black and Hispanic press and general and consumer magazines. This unique publication is used by professional public relations practitioners and professional searchers.

Directories in Print - lists the names and addresses of membership directories of hundreds of trade organizations and professional associations.

Directory of American Libraries With Genealogical and Local History - provides a comprehensive listing of private and public libraries in the US which have genealogical and local history sections. Published by Ancestry.

Directory of Associations - contains the addresses and telephone numbers of thousands of associations in the United States. The associations vary from business oriented, veterans groups, professional and trade and numerous other types. Since many associations have a current address and phone number, this book is a very valuable resource.

Directory of Special Libraries and Information Centers -
lists over 15,000 public libraries and over 19,000 special
libraries, archives, research libraries and information centers
in the United States.

Directory of United States Libraries - lists all of the
libraries in the country. Published by the American Library
Association.

Encyclopedia of Associations - lists over 22,000
professional, vocational, union, hobby and other
associations. Published by Gale Research Company.

*Knowing Where to Look: The Ultimate Guide to
Research* - contains numerous ideas on using libraries.
Written by Lois Horowitz. Available from Writer's Digest
Books.

The National Yellow Book of Funeral Directors - lists
names, addresses and telephone numbers of most funeral
homes and directors in the United States. Listings are by
city, within each state. This is a priceless source of
information for searchers who are attempting to locate
information about a deceased person. Funeral directors
keep files which may list names and addresses of relatives
and friends of the deceased. This is a particularly valuable
resource if an obituary was not published or a death
certificate is not obtainable.

National ZIP Code Directory - in addition to ZIP codes for
every city and town in the nation, this book also identifies
county and civil jurisdictions, as well as their addresses.
Published by the US Postal Service, this book is available
for use or sale at all post offices.

Newspapers in Microform: United States - a helpful reference in locating newspapers stored on microfilm. Published by the Library of Congress.

Peterson's Guide to Four-year Colleges or Accredited Institutions of Post Secondary Education - useful if you wish to obtain the address of an alumni association or a college library. If either group does not have a record of your subject, you may place a "locator notice" in the alumni publication.

Maps and Atlases - often a map is a valuable tool in a search to determine the location of a street or even the location of a city. Libraries have abundant maps that may be useful in your search.

Books which list US Newspapers - there are several books available in libraries which list names, addresses, telephone and FAX numbers of all daily and weekly newspapers in the United States.

Search Related

City Directories and Crisscross Directories - public libraries, especially larger systems, maintain collections of city directories and criss-cross directories of their city and surrounding cities. These two directories can be your best search tools. City directories list individuals in alphabetical order. Criss-cross directories list residents by street in numerical sequence. Begin with the edition for the last year you knew your subject lived in a particular city. Check more current editions to find the last year he is listed and at which address. You can then identify neighbors or former neighbors who might know where the person you are looking for now lives. You can do a computer address update if the address is not over ten years old. Call or write the library and ask them to search for you. In the event they will not search, ask them for names of local researchers to contact. Contact "People Searching News", listed in **Chapter Eight**, for additional information on researchers.

Telephone Books - many libraries maintain collections of old telephone books for their city and surrounding area. These telephone books can provide old addresses of your subject and names and former addresses of spouses, children and other relatives. They are also sources of names of former employers (individual and business names). Use these books in conjunction with your search of city directories.

Biographic Register - annual list (register) of civil service employees published by the Department of State. It includes biographic information on State Department employees as well as personnel of the Agency for International Development, the Peace Corps, the Foreign Agricultural Service, and the United States Information Agency. Many registers include date and place of birth, colleges attended, foreign service posts, and spouse's name.

Birthright: The Guide to Search and Reunion for Adoptees, Birthparents and Adoptive Parents - excellent resource for anyone trying to find a birth parent, adoptive parent or a child who was adopted. Written by Jean A. S. Strauss. Available from Penguin Books.

Dictionary of Surnames - in the event you are not sure of the spelling of a surname, this book by Patrick Hanks and Flavia Hodges has alternate spellings of thousands of surnames. It also explains the origin and meaning of over 70,000 surnames.

Foreign Service Lists - directories of Foreign Service officers are published three times a year by the Department of State. They list field staffs of the US Foreign Service, the US Information Agency, AID, the Peace Corps and the Foreign Agricultural Service. A brief job title appears, as well as date arrived in the country they are assigned and their civil service grade.

How To Locate Anyone Who Is Or Has Been In The Military: Armed Forces Locator Guide - essential resource if the subject of your search is or was in the armed forces. Check your local library for the current edition. Published by MIE Publishing.

Military Officers Registers - excellent resource for obtaining information on individuals who served as officers and warrant officers in the armed forces. Each branch of the service published a register of regular, reserved and retired officers annually. Earlier editions contain name, rank, service number, DOB, colleges and universities attended and some assignment information. Later editions (1968-80) list name, rank, SSN, DOB and other miscellaneous service data. Registers were discontinued in 1981 due to the Privacy Act. Some copies are available on microfiche.

US Air Force Register - annual list of commissioned retired officers -- active and retired. Includes service number (pre mid-1969) or Social Security number and date of birth.

US Army Register - yearly lists of active, reserve and retired officers. Lists service number (pre-mid 1969) or Social Security number and date of birth. Pre 1969 active lists include state of birth and military training.

Register of Commissioned and Warrant Officers - Navy and Marine Corps and Reserve Officers on Active Duty - *of the United States Naval Reserve*

Register of Retired Commissioned and Warrant Officers, Regular and Reserve of the United States Navy and Marine Corps - annual lists that include service number (pre 1972) or Social Security number and date of birth.

Directories of Alumni of the military academies:

Register of Graduates of the United States Air Force Academy has begun to appear in a "condensed" version. The 1989 register is the most recent "complete" version. It contained date of birth, full biographical sketches listing awards, decorations and special honors. Spouse's name and notations indicating most recently known place of employment may appear. Rank, reserve status, year and circumstance of leaving service also may appear. Names of deceased alumni appear in italics. The 1994 Register contains complete historical biographic information.

Register of Graduates and Former Cadets of the United States Military Academy includes state and date of birth. Every effort has been made to include awards, separation dates and ranks, prior military service, colleges and degrees earned, current address and current employment. Deceased graduate's names are printed in italics.

Register of Alumni: Graduates and Former Naval Cadets and Midshipmen includes date and place of birth, last known address, decorations and awards, special assignments, retirements and rank attained. Marine Corps officers are designated. A letter "D" denotes deceased alumni. The name and address of the widow is included, if available.

The MVR Book: Motor Services Guide - describes in detail where and how to obtain driver and vehicle registration records in all states. This is one of the outstanding and easy to use public records research books published by BRB Publications. Check this book before attempting to locate people through state driver license and MVR offices.

Register of Doctors - *The Directory of Medical Specialists by Marquis Who's Who* and *The American Medical Directory* published by the American Medical Association. Medical Associations are excellent resources for locating doctors. State and county medical associations often publish registers and directories of their members. In addition to names, these books also provide information on medical specialty, schooling, business address and other useful information.

The Sourcebook of Federal Courts: US District and Bankruptcy - provides complete information on how to obtain criminal and civil court records and bankruptcy files from federal courts. It outlines the jurisdictions and boundaries of these courts. Federal court records can provide addresses of your subject as well as other individuals who have knowledge of his former and present locations. Published by BRB Publications.

The Sourcebook of State Public Records - explains how to obtain records at the state level for business records, liens and security interest records (UCC), criminal records, workers compensation and vital records, MVR, occupational licensing, and business names and permits. An essential reference book for searchers. Published by BRB Publications.

The Sourcebook of County Asset/Lien Records - a national guide to all county/city government agencies where real estate transactions, UCC financing statement and federal/state tax liens are recorded. Published by BRB Publications.

Who's Who in America - this series of books contains thousands of names and information on prominent people in several different career fields.

Database and Microfilm Information

The following resources have proven to be of immense value to searchers.

Computer Files and Searches - Some larger libraries have the **National Telephone Directory** and the **Social Security Master Death Index** on CD-ROM. The National Telephone Directory contains over 80 million listings of people who have listed telephone numbers. The Social Security Master Death Index lists over 60 million people who have died since 1962. For more detailed explanations of these databases, see **Chapter Ten**.

Draft Registration Records - some libraries have copies of Draft Registration Records of the county where they are located for World War I, II, Korean and Vietnam wars. These records contain legal names, addresses and DOB.

Voter Registration Records - libraries may have access to many years of voter registration lists from the board of elections (voter registration offices) of their local area. Most of these records contain legal names, addresses, DOB and SSN of registered voters.

Microfilm and microfiche files of Real Estate Owners - lists (current and old) of real estate owners are often available in local libraries. This data is usually indexed by name and address.

Newsbank - most libraries have access to local newspaper indexes that may list the name of the person you are seeking. In addition to news articles, names may be listed under announcements such as birth, engagements, marriages, divorces, funeral and death. Many libraries can search national databases available through vendors. Searches can be made for an individual whose name appears in a major newspaper or who may be an officer of a company (even a sole proprietorship). Check with your librarian concerning capabilities for searches and fees.

Newspaper Obituary Files - most libraries maintain an obituary file of local deaths. This information is usually obtained from local newspapers and goes back many years. Most libraries will respond to telephone requests for information from these files. Others will only respond to a written request and some require a search fee. Their response time is usually a few days and some libraries will FAX the requested information. The obituary file is often kept in the information section, however some libraries keep it in their genealogical section.

PHONEFICHE - many libraries have most of the complete telephone directories of cities in the nation on microfiche. In the event the library does not have the National Telephone Directory on CD-ROM, this is a good alternative source of addresses and telephone numbers. The disadvantage is that you must look through each city for listings and addresses. You cannot do a national search with this system as you can with the CD-ROM version of the telephone directories.

Regional Government Depository Libraries

Many libraries are members of the **Regional Government Depository Library Program**. Although public libraries and university libraries usually participate in this program, not all have the facilities for maintaining extensive collections of federal publications. Regional depositories are charged with receiving all new and revised government publications authorized for distribution to depository libraries. Many documents and books published by the federal government and the armed forces may not be available in many libraries. These publications can be acquired from Regional Government Depository Libraries on a loan basis by libraries who participate in this program. Depository libraries are located in every state. Examples of publications that may be available for loan are: armed forces officers registers, Department of State employee registers and lists, federal government telephone books, US government pamphlets on such diverse matters as census data, commercial laws, bankruptcy courts, federal tax matters, etc. Consider using this valuable resource if you are involved with a difficult search. Ask your librarian how to use this service to obtain the publication needed in your search.

The County Courthouse

There are numerous records available at the county courthouse that can provide valuable identifying information. All of this information is in the public domain and is not restricted. These records include:

Boat Registration - Many counties require that pleasure and fishing boats be registered. These records will also have the full name, address and DOB of the owner.

Criminal And Civil Court - All counties keep indefinitely records of all criminal and civil court cases. You can obtain former addresses, physical descriptions, names of the subject's relatives, friends, enemies and lawyers. Ask the clerk for assistance. If your subject has been in trouble with the law, talk to the county sheriff. He may provide information and clues, but be prepared to share any information you have that may be of value to the sheriff's department.

County Vehicle Registration - The county courthouse has the same information concerning registration and licensing of motor vehicles as does the state. While the information is the same, the information in the county courthouse will always be more current. They report to the state monthly or quarterly.

County Business Licenses - Most counties require business licenses. This information is open to the public. It lists names, addresses, other identifying information, and on occasion, the SSN of the owners. Of most importance, it will show the address of the business.

County Vital Statistics - Marriages, divorces, and deaths are all recorded in the county court house. See **Chapter Six** for instructions on how to obtain vital statistics information.

Hunting And Fishing Licenses - Many counties sell hunting and fishing licenses. The records of these licenses will have name, address and DOB of the subject. This information will also be available from the appropriate state agency.

Property Tax - All county courthouses have tax records, especially those related to real estate. They contain the name and address of the owner. In the event your subject owns property, the courthouse will have his current address for tax notices. This is considered public information in every state.

Veteran's Discharges - Most county courthouses register veteran's discharges (DD 214). This is available if the veteran or his family needs this document for state and federal veteran's benefits. These discharges are public information once they are registered. They provide a great deal of information. The most important items are legal name, DOB, SSN, service number, branch and dates of military service.

Public Schools - If your subject has school age children, the public school may be willing to give you the forwarding address of the family or at least the city where they moved. Schools are usually limited as to the amount of information they can provide to the public. High schools often have alumni groups that may have the new address of a former student. High school yearbooks can provide helpful information. These are available in the school library, from alumni groups or, occasionally, in the city public library. Friends and former classmates normally know where their friends have moved. Some may have the new mailing address and telephone number.

Voter Registration Records - In most states, voter registration information is available to the general public. Voter registration files are usually maintained by the county. Some cities also keep a list of voters registered in their municipality. The information available is legal name, address, DOB, political affiliation and SSN in many states. Check your telephone book for voter registration offices. Some libraries may have copies of these records.

City Hall

Useful information is available from city government offices. Most of this is also available from the county and state governments who normally have a great deal more information of value to searchers. Birth records are usually available from the city health department. Sometimes these records can be easily obtained from the city, but are not releasable by the state vital statistics offices. Traffic court and municipal court records are good sources of information. Traffic courts keep accident reports as well as ticket information. These records will list name, address, vehicle information and physical description. In smaller cities, ask to speak to the chief of police if the situation warrants. Building permits and pet permits are kept by city governments.

City Utility Services

Most cities operate garbage pickup, water, sewer and electrical utility services. The utilities have records of customers that include their address. In accordance with most state open-records laws, these addresses are considered public information. However, some cities and states may restrict the release of information at the customers request. When a customer moves, they will often give the new address to the utility, so their deposit can be returned.

Chapter Eight

Where To Obtain Information And Assistance From Non-Government Sources

It is possible to obtain assistance and identifying information through non-government activities, private organizations, businesses, private individuals and other sources.

Adoptee And Birth Parent Search Organizations

If you are searching for a birth parent or for a child who was given up for adoption, contact one of the national birth parent search groups. **Do this whether or not know the name of the subject.** These organizations have years of experience in every phase of the search process. They are extremely familiar with adoption laws and the means to obtain identifying information to solve this type of search. Some of these organizations require that you become a member before you can receive any information or assistance. Once you have obtained a name (or a first name and DOB), use the methods in this book to locate the person.

The American Adoption Congress   (202) 483-3399
1000 Connecticut Ave NW, Suite 9
Washington, DC 20036

Adoptee Reunion Registries

Adoptee reunion registries attempt to bring together adoptees and their birth parents. This is done by registering identifying information such as DOB, place of birth and other information that would assist in identifying a person who was adopted. This registry system is used by both adoptees and birth parents who are attempting to be reunited with their blood relatives. There are numerous registers throughout the nation. Most are local in coverage. The two major national organizations are:

International Soundex Reunion Registry   (702) 882-7755
(ISSR)
PO Box 2312
Carson City, NV 89702-2312

Adoptees Liberty Movement Assn   (212) 581-1568
(ALMA)   FAX (212) 765-2861
200 Madison Avenue
New York, NY 10016

American Medical Association

Two medical directories list the names and current addresses of physicians. They are *The Directory of Medical Specialists*, by Marquis Who's Who and *The American Medical Directory* by the American Medical Association.

Both references list a doctor's medical specialty and type of practice. The *Directory of Medical Specialists* also provides biographical information, such as education and military service. Both directories can usually be found in large public libraries. Another useful source in locating physicians is the American Medical Association's computer data file in Chicago. You can request the address of a physician by writing:

Data Release   (312) 464-5199
American Medical Association
535 North Dearborn St.
Chicago, IL 60610

Attorney/Investigator

Charles Eric Gordon is an attorney concentrating on locating persons who have been missing for a substantial period of time or about whom little information is known. He is a consultant to law firms, corporations, government agencies and foreign governments in tracing witnesses, heirs, beneficiaries, relatives, debtors and others. He will counsel individuals about difficult or unusual cases.

Mr. Gordon has world-wide contacts and many years of experience as both an attorney and an investigator. He can also assist in acquiring information and public records that are difficult to access: e.g., vital records, voter registration and court records.

Charles Eric Gordon, Esq.   (516) 433-5065
5 Joyce Road
PO Box 514
Plainview, NY 11803-0514

Banks, Credit Unions
And Insurance Companies

As a public service, many banks, credit unions and insurance companies (automobile, life and home owners) will forward letters to their current and former customers. If you know the current or former financial institution of the person you are looking for, this may be an excellent way to contact them. Before attempting this, contact the institution to ensure that they will forward your letter or provide an address. Some companies provide this service for their members/customers only. If you forward a letter, be sure to include your return address on the envelope. If the subject has moved, you might obtain their current address. See "US Postal Service" in **Chapter Five** for details.

Cable Television Companies

Most cable television stations operate under state laws that are similar to the ones that apply to city utilities. These laws allow cable television companies to release names and addresses of customers to the public, unless the customer requests otherwise. Since most people subscribe to cable television, this is an excellent source to obtain a subject's address.

Churches

Churches can be of great assistance in many searches. Most priests, ministers and rabbis know the addresses of their current and former members. Most churches and synagogues maintain records of membership, baptisms, confirmations, first communions, bar mitzvahs, weddings and burials. Many religious groups have church sponsored clubs and organizations which should be contacted for information. Contact other members of the church that the subject attended. If you know the religious affiliation of the person, this can be a valuable place to obtain addresses and information (e.g., date of birth, former address, information concerning divorces, names and addresses of friends, relatives and former spouses).

The Salvation Army

The Salvation Army conducts searches of missing people for immediate family members only through their national missing persons network. Contact the local Salvation Army Social Service Center for information and a registration form. There is a $10.00 fee for this service.

There are four Salvation Army territorial headquarters with Missing Person Services that can assist in a search. Their addresses are as follows:

Southern US Salvation Army
Missing Persons Services
1424 NE Expressway
Atlanta, GA 30329

Western US Salvation Army
Missing Persons Service
30840 Hawthorne Boulevard
Rancho Palos Verdes, CA 90274

Eastern US Salvation Army
Missing Persons Services
120 W 14th Street
New York, NY 10011

Central US Salvation Army
Missing Persons Services
860 N Dearborn Street
Chicago, IL 60610

Civic, Fraternal And Ethnic Organizations

There are numerous local chapters of national organizations and clubs such as the Lions, Elks, Order of the Moose, Rotarians, Masons and Shriners. There are also historical and patriotic societies and ethnic societies and clubs. These organizations have both national headquarters and local chapters, both of which can assist in your search. See the local telephone book or ask your librarian for addresses and telephone numbers.

Colleges, Universities And Alumni Associations

The federal Family and Educational Rights and Privacy Act allows colleges and universities to release "directory information" to the public without the consent of the student. A student may request that all or part of this information be withheld from the public by making a written request to do so (but few do). "Directory Information" includes, but is not limited to, student's name, current address, telephone listing, major, date and place of birth, dates of attendance, degrees and awards received and previous educational agencies or institutions attended. Some colleges may release a student's SSN. Contact college registrars for this information.

College alumni associations try to keep current addresses of former students and most will either provide the address or will forward a letter. They also publish directories of former students (some list graduates only) with current addresses and employment. If the alumni association will not give an address, contact the college library, which will have a copy of the directory. They normally will provide an address or other identifying information. Alumni associations and college libraries will also have copies of yearbooks that can sometimes provide the individual's legal name, hometown, degree and other information. See *Peterson's Guide to Four-year Colleges or Accredited Institutions of Post Secondary Education* for additional information on this subject in the "Libraries" section of **Chapter Seven**.

Genealogical Libraries

The **Church of Jesus Christ of Latter-day Saints** (Mormons) has the largest family history (genealogical) library in the world. They operate numerous local family history libraries in major cities throughout the United States. Local libraries can obtain endless amounts of genealogical information from the main library in Salt Lake City. Local libraries are extremely helpful to searchers. Many libraries have the Social Security Master Death Index, local birth and death records and excellent collections of local telephone books. For additional information, contact the nearest local family history library or write:

Church of Jesus Christ of Latter-day Saints
Family History Department   (801) 240-2584
35 North West Temple
Salt Lake City, UT 84150

Genealogical Researchers

Use of the services of professional genealogical researchers is strongly recommended in many cases. These researchers can obtain valuable information from census records (federal, state, local and military) as well as family histories, vital records, historical and patriotic and genealogical societies. Most professional genealogists specialize in a certain area of intense expertise, such as ethnic groups, military or a select geographical area. The fees normally charged for their services are moderate and are well worth the excellent services they provide. For assistance in locating a professional genealogist for your particular needs contact your local library, (genealogical section), the local Latter-day saints (LDS) Family History Library or the yellow pages of your telephone book. Or contact:

Association of Professional Genealogists
3421 M St NW, #236
Washington, DC 20007

Local Merchants And Businesses

Local merchants and businesses can often provide valuable information about the person you are looking for. Everyone purchases food and beverages, and uses services such as dry cleaners and laundries, restaurants, auto repair shops, etc. By contacting local merchants and businesses close to where the subject once lived, you may be able to obtain excellent information about your subject.

National Association Of Investigative Specialists

The National Association of Investigative Specialists is a world-wide network of private investigative professionals and/or agencies. With over 1,500 members, it is one of the largest associations in the world for private investigators. For a free referral, contact:

National Association of   (512) 928-8190
    Investigative Specialists
PO Box 33244
Austin, TX 78764

The National Reunion Registry

The National Reunion Registry is a database of over 6,000 military reunion organizations and reunion planners, a valuable resource if you are searching for a veteran. If you know what military unit or ship the veteran served with, contact the Registry to determine if there is an appropriate reunion organization. This is an excellent means to locate the veteran or someone who knows him/her. Send a self-addressed stamped envelope:

National Reunion Registry   (210) 438-4177
    and Press Service   FAX (210) 438-4114
PO Box 355
Bulverde, TX 78163-0355

The Nationwide Locator

The Nationwide Locator provides numerous computer search services to facilitate locating individuals. These searches include the SSN trace, address updates, surname searches, telephone number ownership, death index and date of birth searches.

The Nationwide Locator is owned by Military Information Enterprises, Inc. which is a member of the San Antonio Retail Merchants Association and is listed by Dun and Bradstreet. It has been in business since 1988. All searches are described in **Chapter Ten**. For a free brochure write or FAX:

The Nationwide Locator   FAX (210) 828-4667
PO Box 39903
San Antonio, TX 78218

Newspapers And Magazines

Local newspapers are valuable tools for locating individuals. Select one with the greatest circulation in the city where the subject last lived. Visit your local library for a copy of *Gale's Directory of Publications,* or a similar publication, for names, addresses and telephone numbers of newspapers in the United States. Place an advertisement in the personal section similar to the following.

Joe L James
Urgent, anyone who knows
his current location: call collect
(555) 555-5555

Thousands of people read the classified section and you may get a quick response. A letter to the editor of a small town newspaper may bring some help in your search. Newspapers in metropolitan areas often publish "letters to the editor" which can be useful. Consider contacting a reporter at the newspaper and ask him to do an article on your search. This can bring a lot of leads or even a solution.

Newspapers may have archives where previously published papers are kept. These can be of immense assistance in locating someone. The obituaries of a subject's relative can provide names and residences of the widow (or widower), children, other relatives and friends of the deceased. There is usually a small fee for copies of obituaries. Obituaries may also be available at the city library (see **Chapter Seven**). Newspapers publish information on births, marriages, divorces, engagements, wedding anniversaries, family reunions, legal notices, military news, news of social and civic organizations and churches.

People Searching News (PSN) is an excellent magazine with emphasis on adoption and missing person searches ($18.00 for six issues per year; sample copy + registry forms is $6.95). *PSN* sells a variety of search books and can offer the services of more than 1,000 researchers world-wide. *PSN* also has a large "in-search-of" classified ad section; subscribers are likely to offer you help and information. Their address and no-fee search hot-line is:

People Searching News   (407) 768-2222
PO Box 100444
Palm Bay, FL 32910-0444

Reunions Magazine is the only publication in the nation that concentrates on reunions of all kinds. In addition to articles on searching and genealogical research, it provides tips, leads and hints to help search for missing people. Other articles focus on adoptees and birth parents searches. To subscribe ($24.00 per year) or for a sample copy, send $2.00 to:

Reunions Magazine   (414) 263-4567
PO Box 11727   FAX (414) 263-6331
Milwaukee, WI 53211   Reunions1@aol.com

On-Line Computer Services

Computer owners who subscribe to CompuServe can use the telephone directory service. This service is similar to the National Telephone Directory which is described in **Chapter Ten**. It provides the name of people who have listed telephone numbers along with their addresses. Additional information about on-line computer services for professional searchers is contained in **Chapter Ten**.

Individuals who subscribe to on-line computer services can use bulletin boards and forums to solicit help and information in their searches.

America On-Line	(800) 827-6364
CompuServe	(800) 848-8990
Delphi	(800) 695-4005
Genie	(800) 638-9636
Prodigy	(800) 776-3449

People Who Are Due Unclaimed Assets

There are numerous companies that search for people who are heirs or who are eligible to receive unclaimed assets held by probate courts and state unclaimed property offices. These companies receive a percentage of all money recovered by the persons they locate. Contact the author of this book if unclaimed assets are involved. The author searches for people due unclaimed assets and has located individuals who have received millions of dollars of inheritances and other unclaimed money. See **Chapter Twelve** for information and address.

Political Organizations

If your subject was active in politics, contact the local political organizations where he last lived. In addition to the local organization, you may get some leads from the state organizations. The telephone book and the library are again your best sources to obtain addresses and telephone numbers of political groups.

Private Investigators

Some difficult cases may need the help of a professional investigator. There are numerous investigators listed in local telephone books. Before you enter into an agreement for their services, determine if they have experience in locating missing people and have access to on-line computer services. They should be able to do SSN searches, address updates, US Postal Change of Address file updates, SSN death index searches, the National Telephone Directory searches and Date of Birth searches. These computer searches are described in **Chapter Ten**.

Professional And Trade Associations

Information is provided in Chapter Six on how to locate professional people through state regulating agencies. These people may also be located through local offices. As an example, doctors may be located through the County Medical Societies. Attorneys may be located through city and county bar associations. The same is true for other professionals or merchants. If you know the last city they lived in and their profession, find out if there is a local chapter or office for that particular group. This can be easily done by looking in the yellow pages of that city's telephone directory or by contacting the information section of the appropriate city library. You may also use the *Directory of Associations* in your local library to get telephone numbers and addresses of national headquarters of professional associations.

Telephone Company

Contact your local telephone company and ask if they have copies of out of town telephone books, especially if the local library does not have the one you need.

The directory assistance (long distance information) operator can give valuable information, in addition to telephone numbers. Request the information operator check the entire area code for the person you are seeking. Most area code operators will do this search. Dial 1 (area code) 555-1212.

MCI has directory assistance service to locate both domestic and international telephone numbers with a single call. For 75¢, you can request two telephone numbers if you provide the name and city, domestic or international, of the person you want to call. Use of the traditional directory assistance as described above requires dialing directory assistance in any of the 144 area codes in the US. The MCI directory service is available to the public by calling 1 (800) CALL-INFO (1 (800) 225-5463).

In some areas you may obtain an address or verify if a person has a phone--even if the number is unlisted. There are different rules in each state and area code concerning unlisted telephone numbers. If the person sought does have an unlisted number, call the operator and have them call the person and ask them to contact you. In some areas, this service is done only for emergencies or important matters, so inform the operator of its importance. Many people can be located easily through the telephone company or telephone books.

Television And Radio Programs

If you have a unique situation or a good human interest story, you might get local or national television or radio stations to do a "story" about your search. Call or write the appropriate program or segment producer. Be sure to mention this book as it may give your story additional national appeal. Your library can provide telephone numbers and addresses of both local and national programs and stations. Contact the major networks at:

ABC	(212) 456-7777
CBS	(212) 975-4321
CNN	(404) 827-1500
FOX	(213) 856-1000
NBC	(212) 664-4444

Veteran Organizations

There are 27 million living veterans. If your subject is a veteran, retired from one of the military services, or a member of the reserve or National Guard, there are numerous groups and organizations that you can contact for assistance. Many major organizations have both national and local chapters. Some examples are: **The American Legion, Veterans of Foreign Wars** (VFW), **Disabled American Veterans** (DAV), **AMVETS**, the **Retired Officers Association** (TROA), the **Reserve Officers Association** (ROA), the **Non-Commissioned Officers Association** (NCOA) and the **Chief Petty Officers Association** (CPOA).

Their national headquarters will either provide an address or forward a letter. Local chapters will usually provide a great deal of information, if the person is or was a member. Check the yellow pages of the telephone book where your subject last lived. It is strongly recommended that you use the book *How to Locate Anyone Who Is Or Has Been In The Military: Armed Forces Locator Guide.* The order form is at the end of this book.

Chapter Nine

Determining If
The Person Is Deceased

Sometimes it is best to determine if the person you are looking for is deceased. There is a good possibility the person may be deceased if they were born over 60 years ago, if you have not heard from them for many years, if their employment was in a hazardous industry or profession, or if they may have been killed in a war while in military service. No matter what their age, it is usually fairly easy to determine if a person is deceased.

If you know the first and last name of the individual and approximately when they were born, you can look them up on **Social Security Master Death Index**. (See **Chapter Ten** and later in this chapter.)

Each state maintains manual and computer indexes of people who have died in their state. This information is usually available to the public. Some states have "closed records" and will only provide information to family members. **Chapter Six** has the addresses of the state offices which provide death certificates.

Former employers, social, civic and veteran organizations also have information on the death of former members and employees.

Most libraries and newspaper archives keep copies of obituaries that were published when an individual died. These obituaries may be available at the funeral home that arranged for the burial of the individual. However, obituaries are not published on everyone who dies. Libraries have books that list addresses and telephone numbers of all newspapers, funeral homes and morticians in the United States.

Each military service has a casualty branch. They can provide copies of casualty reports or certain information on people who died on active duty or in retired status. Contact the following for more information:

Air Force	(210) 652-5513
Army	(703) 325-5300
Marines	(703) 696-2069
Navy	(800) 443-9297

Remember, if your have not heard from the person for many years and all other searches have failed to produce positive results, it may be wise to determine if this person is deceased. Make this determination before spending a lot of time and money. The following agencies may be able to help you.

American Battle Monuments Commission

The American Battle Monuments Commission (ABMC) can provide the names of 124,912 US war dead of World War I and II who are interred in American burial grounds in foreign countries. They can also provide the names of any of 94,093 US servicemen and women who were missing in action or lost or buried at sea during World War I, World

War II, the Korean and Vietnam Wars. For further
information contact:

American Battle Monuments Commission (202) 761-0532
Pulaski Building, Room 5127   (202) 761-0537
20 Massachusetts Ave, NW   FAX (202) 761-1375
Washington, DC 20314-0001

Department Of Veterans Affairs

The Department of Veterans Affairs (VA) maintains
extremely accurate death information on their computer
database of over 60 million veterans. This information is
available to anyone by telephone or letter (see **Chapter
Five** for details).

The VA will disclose if a veteran identified in their files is
deceased. They will also give his date of death, service
number and SSN. The VA is informed of a veteran's death
by funeral homes, family members and other government
agencies and have excellent records in this regard. Call any
VA Regional Office for assistance at (800) 827-1000.

The National Cemetery System is a branch of the
Department of Veterans Affairs. They provide burial
location assistance to the next of kin or close friends of the
deceased. VA staff members can research records to
determine if a specific decedent is interred in one of the VA
National Cemeteries.

To request a burial search on a specific individual, include
as much of the following information as possible:

1. full name (first, middle, and last)
2. date and place of birth
3. date and place of death

4. state from which entered military service

5. rank and military unit in which served on active duty

No form is required and no fee is charged for this service. Send the above information to:

Department of Veterans Affairs   (202) 273-5225
National Cemetery System   FAX (202) 273-6697
Director of Field Operations
810 Vermont Avenue, NW
Washington, DC 20420

The National Archives

The National Archives and other federal agencies have casualty information. The following is a list of military computer casualty records maintained by the National Archives. These records are available to the public in either computer formats or in printouts.

Korean Conflict Casualty File - contains data of all US Military personnel who died by hostile means as a result of combat duty in the Korean conflict. There are 32,642 records with names, service numbers and dates of death from 1950-57.

Southeast Asia Combat Area Casualties Database - contains 58,152 records of all US Military personnel who died as a result of hostilities or other causes in Cambodia, China, Laos, North Vietnam, South Vietnam or Thailand from 1957-89.

Korean War Casualty File-US Army - contains 109,975 records of both fatal and non-fatal Army casualties.

The Casualty Information System - for the periods 1961-1981 contains records of casualties suffered by all US Army personnel and their dependents. Extracts of records for all US Army active duty personnel who have died are available.

All requests for copies of records must be received in writing and be accompanied by full payment. For fee and information requirements, contact:

Center for Electronic Records (NSX)   (301) 713-6630
Nat'l Archives and Records Administration
8601 Adelphi Road   FAX (301) 713-6911
College Park, MD 20740-6001

Social Security Administration

The Social Security Administration will verify if they have a report of death of an individual in their files. Call the Social Security Administration at **(800) 772-1213**. Provide the individual's name and SSN or DOB (it is helpful to have the name of the individual's parents). You will be told if they have a report of the individual being deceased. If deceased, the SSA can give the date of death and ZIP code of place of death and ZIP code where benefits were mailed.

The SSA has created a **Master Death Index**. The index includes everyone reported to the SSA that has died since 1962. The SSA Master Death Index lists first and last name, SSN, DOB, date of death, ZIP code of the last known address of the individual and the ZIP code where any death benefits were mailed. The SSA sells copies of their **Master Death Index** computer file to information brokers and credit bureaus (Trans Union, TRW, CBI). Many genealogical researchers, private investigators and heir searchers also have copies of the SSA Master Death Index. It is available for use by the general public in many main public libraries and family history libraries. If you know the first and last name of the individual and approximately when they were born, you can look them up on the index.

Searchers can receive some valuable information from a deceased person's original Social Security card application. It lists name, address, employer at time of application, SSN, birth date, birthplace, parents and original signature. This information may assist in locating the decedent's children. Request Form SS-5. Return the form with $7.00 if SSN is known; or $16.00 if unknown. For request with unknown SSN, list as much information about the person as possible. Write to:

Freedom of Information Staff   (800) 772-1213
4-C-5 Annex Building
6401 Security Boulevard
Baltimore, MD 21235

Chapter Ten

Computer Searches
And Access Packages

There are several computer searches and access packages that are available directly or indirectly to the general public. These are the searches used by professionals such as collection agencies, private investigators, attorneys, estate (heir) searchers and locator services. The general public may use these searches directly by going "on-line" if they have a computer and pay set-up fees and search charges. If you are looking for only a few people or it is not feasible for you to go on-line, the services of a locator or a private investigator are recommended.

Computer Searches

These are the major computer searches used to locate individuals:

- Social Security number trace
- Criss-cross or reverse search
- Date of birth search
- Address update
- Surname search
- Telephone number ownership (residential)
- Driver license search

If using a locator service or a private investigator, the retail price for these searches range from $30.00 to $150.00 per search.

Social Security Number Trace

A SSN trace is used to obtain an individual's current address. This is accomplished by running a SSN against the "header information" contained in a credit bureau database. With a simple SSN trace, 87 to 95 percent of people can be quickly located.

A credit database is made up of credit files. Everyone who uses credit has a credit file. A credit file is updated each time a person uses credit to buy a house or a car, rent an apartment, or make any purchase using a credit card. A credit file can contain a person's full name, SSN, age, date or year of birth, current address, former address, dates addresses were reported, credit history and sometimes employer and name of spouse. Everything but the credit history is "header information". When a SSN trace is run, only this header information is given. The Fair Credit Reporting Act prohibits obtaining credit history information except for authorized reasons. Locating people is never considered an acceptable reason to access credit history.

Sometimes when a SSN trace is run, the name and SSN are checked against the SSA Master Death Index. If the individual is on this index, their month and year of death will be listed on the SSN trace.

There are three credit bureaus: Trans Union, CBI-Equifax and TRW. Each of these bureaus has its own credit database. These three bureaus combined have over 300 million individual credit files which are updated daily. Some people have files in one or two and occasionally all three of these credit databases. These are the most valuable resources in locating people. They are frequently used by collection agencies, private investigators and many reunion and alumni organizations. These groups usually gain access to a credit database through a local dealer or a credit reporting agency in their community.

The following are examples of all three Credit bureau SSN traces.

```
                        TRANS UNION

* SOCIAL SECURITY NUMBER TRACE *          123-45-6789

   NAME/SPOUSE                              SSN OWNER
   ADDRESS                               ADDR RPT DATE

1. DOE, JOSEPH E  /JANE                      SUBJECT
   9980  POB 9980, DEL RIO NM.,  87422         11/94
   2224  E DURANGO, SANTA FE NM.,A 124, 87346  08/87
   1212  POB 1212, LOS SANTOS NM., 87921       10/84


*** HAWK-ALERT:  CLEAR
*** END OF NETWORK

================== END OF REPORT  ===============
```

```
                         TRW
                SOCIAL SECURITY TRACE

SSN:  123-45-6789
INPUT SSN ISSUED 1977-1979
JOHN D DOE                         SSN:  123-45-6789
 PO BOX 6754                       YOB:  1964
 SEATTLE WA  98220
 RPTD:  9-94
JOHN D DOE                         SSN:  123-45-6789
 3524 1ST AVE N
 SEATTLE WA  98324
 FIRST RPTD:  11-92
```

```
ABBREVIATED NAME/ADDRESS:
JOHN D DOE                        SSN: 123-45-6789
 3524 1 98324
NOT TO BE USED FOR CREDIT GRANTING
MAY CONTAIN INFORMATION FOR MORE THAN ONE
CONSUMER
END --
================= END OF REPORT ==================
```

```
                    CBI-Equafax
              SOCIAL SECURITY TRACE

    SSN ISSUED -77  STATE ISSUED-NY

M1 OF 2
Name - DOE, JOHN, D
Address - PO BOX 6754,SEATTLE, WA, 98220, 09/94
Former Address - 3524 1ST AVE N, SEATTLE WA  98324, 11/94,
Employment  - , STEVES & SONS
     SS- 123-45-6789   AGE  30

M2 OF 2
Name ---- DOE,-GEANNIE D,
Address - PO BOX 6754,SEATTLE, WA, 98220, 09/94
Former Address - 3524 1ST AVE N, SEATTLE WA  98324, 11/94,
     SS-123-45-6789
 FN - SMITH, GEANNIE D
```

Criss-Cross Search

A criss-cross search will return the "header information" contained in the individual's credit file, as in a SSN trace. However, instead of entering a SSN to obtain a name and address, a name and address are entered to obtain a SSN or DOB. You can even enter an old address and receive a more current address. You may be required to enter a DOB or SSN. If known, these identifiers should be used. The information provided from the reverse report is the same as that provided in a SSN trace report as shown above. All three credit bureaus have criss-cross searches available.

Date of Birth Search

There are several proprietary databases that include, and are therefore accessed by, date of birth information. Many of these databases contain over 160 million records. Each record can contain names, addresses, DOB, SSN as well as other pertinent information. These databases are composed of driver license, voter registration and marketing information, national magazine subscription files, city directory files and credit file header information, as well as state and national death information.

A search may be conducted by providing:

1. a full name and a DOB and SSN, if known.

2. a full name and an approximate DOB or age range.

3. a first or last name and an exact date of birth.

The results will depend upon what information is contained in the individual record. The record may contain only a city and state of residence, or it may contain a complete address and physical characteristics.

This is an ideal search for women who may have changed their names, children who have been adopted or men who have changed their surname.

Address Update

Sometimes the address you have will not be the most current one, even if it is acquired from a SSN or DOB computer search. The best way to be sure an address is current is to request a computer address update. Trans Union has a separate database derived from sources other than credit information: city directory files, some state driver license files, marketing and major magazine subscription information, the US Post Office Change of Address file and other commercial datafiles. These are all excellent files and are updated on a regular basis.

To receive an address update, enter the individual's name and last known address. The returned information will include one of the following:

1. The individual's name, most current reported address and telephone number.

2. The same name and address as input if there is not a more current one on the computer file. The telephone number will also be included.

3. No information on the individual of he/she has moved and there is no forwarding address on the computer file.

The telephone number reported may be an "unlisted" one, or one that is not available in other files like the National Telephone Directory.

The disadvantage to this search is that if the person lived in a large apartment complex, the search will usually only return neighbors, not a more current address. **This search is not recommended for PO Box and Rural Route addresses.**

The advantage to the Address Update search is you can request the name, address and telephone number of up to 20 neighbors. Even if a more current address is not obtained, contacting a neighbor can provide valuable information.

The following is an example of Trans Union's address update search:

TRANS UNION SUBJECT VERIFICATION REPORT

DATE: 08-22-1994   TIME: 13:16:18   SUBJECT ID: SV05

SV05I1 ROBERTS,DAVID,C*
573,,LINDEN PLACE,,,BUFFALO GAP,TX,79606,*

SUBJECT VERIFICATION WITH 5 NEIGHBORS

ADDRESS

01. ROBERTS,DAVID,C   DU: SFDU   DOR:1992   (908) 585-8012
85   SPRING   CT   EATONTOWN   NJ 07724

NEIGHBORS

01. LEVINE WADE   DU: SFDU   DOR:1992   (908) 389-5274
89   SPRING   CT   EATONTOWN   NJ 07724

02. PERKINS STEVE   DU: DUPLEX   DOR:1993   (908) 358-8447
88   SPRING   CT   EATONTOWN   NJ 07724

03. MATTHEW K F   DU: SFDU   DOR:1988   (908) 594-8493
93   SPRING   CT   EATONTOWN   NJ 07724

04. GRAZETTE D   DU: DUPLEX   DOR:1988   (908) 892-5492
83   SPRING   CT   EATONTOWN   NJ 07724

05. STONE CHAD   DU: DUPLEX   DOR:1987   (908) 938-5964
80   SPRING   CT   EATONTOWN   NJ 07724

END OF ATLAS REPORT

Surname Search

If the only information available is a name, request a surname (last name) search. This will give a list of names, addresses and telephone numbers of people with that name. If the surname is unusual, even if it does not list a matching first name, a person with that surname might be a relative.

CompuServe offers an on-line surname search which provides name, address and telephone number. The database will search one state at a time.

Metronet offers a nationwide surname search. This database will provide a list of matching names along with the address, city, state, ZIP code, telephone number and months of residence.

Trans Union also offers a surname search. However, it can only search by surname and first initial. An address, DOB, or a former address are not required. The search can be nationwide or it can be confined to a specific state, city or ZIP code. Since only an initial can be entered instead of a first name, the effectiveness of this search is reduced. This search is of little value for a common name such as Smith or Jones.

The **National Telephone Directory** is a file contained on CD-ROM discs. This is not an on-line database, but it is accessed by computer and a special CD reader. At the present time, there are two major files marketed. Both have approximately 80 million names, addresses and telephone numbers. One contains the information from the white pages of most telephone directories published in the United States. The other is a combination of telephone book information and marketing information. Both files are not entirely current nor are they highly accurate. These files are relatively inexpensive and are a good source of information to reunion organizers, private investigators, etc. Many are available for use in public libraries. The accuracy of both files is approximately 80 percent.

Searches may be limited to particular states, cities or ZIP codes. Reverse searches are also available. You may search for the owner of a telephone number or the resident of a certain address. You can also obtain a list of neighbors with their addresses and telephone numbers.

The following is an example of a surname search from the National Telephone Directory:

Brigs, Alice 151 Cedar Lake Rd, Hopkinsville, TN 75305
    629-564-2801
Brigs, Cheryl 55 Welcome, Minneapolis, MN 55429
    206-573-9142
Brigs, Dennis 424 Bluebell St, Moorehead, MT 86560
    818-233-0459
Brigs, Gary E 867 Sunshadow Lane, Austin, TX 78711
    512-420-2383
Brigs, John G 615 Broadman Rd, Brookville, NH 16477
    723-785-4401
Brigs, Mark 281 W Lanark Ave, Camden, KY 45038
    418-734-8690
Brigs, N A 5174 Nelson, Danbury, OK 66726
    308-217-1348
Brigs, P 13860 Dreamwood St, Franklin, GA 38233
    610-655-7577
Brigs, Sharon 18690 81st Ave N, Osseo, ND 65511
    712-204-2383
Brigs, Tony A 6504 116 1/2 Ave N, Champlin, NE 85316
    212-274-3948

Telephone Number Ownership (Residential)

If you have a telephone number of an individual (not a business) and want to find the name and address of the owner, Trans Union can provide this information. When a telephone number and area code are entered into the program, the current owner will be provided along with their address, if this information is in the file. This search is often used by collection agencies and private investigators to confirm an individual's current address. The address provided is often that of a relative or a friend.

If the number entered is for a business or is unlisted, no information will be returned.

State Driver License And MVR Files

Several states provide on-line access to their driver license and motor vehicle registration files. With a full name and a date of birth, a search of the driver license database can provide the name and address of individuals who have a driver license or an identification card in that state. With a full name or a vehicle identification number (VIN number), a search of the motor vehicle database can provide the owner's name, address and other vehicles owned. These files are excellent sources for addresses of individuals, if you know the specific state where they live. Searches for addresses can be performed with name and DOB, or driver license number and by name only in most states (surname searches). Many researchers and investigators subscribe to state services, particularly if their searches are limited to a particular state.

A computer search of driver license files is not always recommended. Each state has their own rules and fees (see **Chapter Six**). As of yet, there is not a national database with the complete information from all 50 states. So if you are not sure of the state, you will have to search state by state until you find something. That can get very costly. Even if you do find an address, it may not be current. People often move and do not want to go to the expense and hassle of changing the address on their driver license each time.

Another factor to consider is that some of the computer databases are very restrictive. If you are looking for Donald James O'Connor and he is registered as Donald J. O'Connor, the search may not come back with a match even though he is in the database. Because of the abundance of other data sources, we do not recommend attempting a driver license source until you have tried the other searches first.

Computer Access Packages

The following computer on-line access packages are for use by professional searchers, alumni groups, reunions planners, etc. They are not intended for individuals who are only searching for a few people.

The Nationwide Locator
Direct Access Package

The *Nationwide Locator Direct Access Package* is a low cost program that provides access to the Trans Union database. This program enables you to obtain addresses of people at the lowest possible price. There are no restrictions as to who can use the Nationwide Locator Direct Access Package. The database does not provide any credit information or credit reports. None of the information provided is regulated by the Fair Credit Reporting Act. This access package includes six major categories of searches and a total of 22 different search combinations.

- Social Security number trace
- Social Security number retrace (criss-cross)
- Address update
- Subject verification
- Surname search
- Telephone number ownership

All searches are on-line and you receive instant responses. Most searches are **$6.00** each. Social Security traces and reverse traces are less with volume usage.

Some advantages of this program are:

- 24 hour a day access
- Instant reports
- No large up-front fee
- No line charge
- No minimum usage requirements
- No monthly user fee
- User friendly access program

An IBM compatible computer, a modem, a telephone and a major credit card (VISA, MasterCard or American Express) are the only requirements. The cost of this package is **$290.00**.

The NIS On-Line
Information Services

The *NIS On-Line Information Services* is the nation's most versatile computer access package. This package provides access to the files of all major information databases. This package is used by hundreds of private investigators, researchers and other professionals. Some of the available searches are:

- Address update
- Asset searches
- Atlas surname search
- Bank asset locate search
- Canadian MVR search
- Celebrity address search
- College degree verification

- Commercial credit
- Criminal history
- Driver license traces
- Federal court records
- Government contracts search
- Media/periodical quick scan
- Motor vehicle registration traces
- National aircraft search
- National change of address
- National criss-cross
- National pilot registration
- Newspaper library search
- Post Office Box information
- Postal forwarding
- Professional license verification
- Real estate databases
- Real property search
- Social Security Master Death Index
- Social Security searches
- SSN reverse searches (national identifier)
- State driver license conviction searches
- State driver license search
- State MVR searches
- Subject affiliations
- Subject verification
- Surname search by DOB
- Surname searches
- Tax databases
- Telephone number look-up
- US company profile (Dun & Bradstreet)
- Utility search
- Vessel registration
- Worker's compensation

The cost of each search varies. Most searches give instant on-line results, while some searches will be returned within 3-5 days. You do not need a computer to use this program. It can be accessed by phone, FAX or mail.

The NIS On-Line Information Services is user friendly, menu driven, available 24 hours a day and accessible by phone, mail, FAX and E-mail. The cost of this package is **$395.00**. You can be on-line within 3-5 days.

To request a brochure of either of these access packages, write or FAX:

The Nationwide Locator   FAX (210) 828-4667
PO Box 39903
San Antonio, Texas 78218

For Individual Searches

The Nationwide Locator will provide names, addresses and other important information from many different databases containing millions of records. This information is available to friends and relatives, attorneys, private investigators, collection agencies, reunion planners and others. Our data is highly accurate and reasonably priced. The Nationwide Locator is operated by the author.

Social Security search
Provide a name and the nine digit Social Security number (SSN) and we will provide the person's most current reported address, date reported and all previous reported addresses, if this number is contained in a national credit file. If a report of death has been submitted, it will be listed. **$30.00** per SSN for a nationwide search.

Address update
Provide the name and last known address (not over ten years old) and we will provide the most current reported

address and the names and telephone numbers of five neighbors. **$30.00** per name submitted.

National Surname search

Provide the first name, middle initial and last name and we will use the National Telephone Directory to provide the names, addresses and listed telephone numbers of everyone in the nation with a matching name. **$30.00** per name submitted.

Date of Birth search

Provide first and last name, approximate date or year of birth and Social Security number (if known) and we will provide all matching names, city and state of residence. May be able to provide street address and phone number. **$75.00** per name and date of birth submitted.

Social Security Death Index search

Provide either the name and date of birth, name and Social Security number or name only and we will provide a list of people who are deceased, their SSN, date of birth, and the date and place of death as reported by the Social Security Administration. **$30.00** per name.

Search results will be provided to you within 24 hours of receipt. This will be returned by mail or by FAX if requested. Volume discounts are available. Prices are subject to change without notice. Other specialized searches are available. **Texas residents add 7.75% tax.**

Client agrees that all information obtained through the Nationwide Locator will be used for lawful purposes and agrees to hold the Nationwide Locator harmless for any use of this service. Client states that the client understands and agrees the Nationwide Locator does not warrant and does not guarantee information obtained from database searches. Client agrees to pay for all searches made by the Nationwide Locator regardless of results (to include "no record"). The Nationwide Locator is owned by Military Information Enterprises, Inc., is a member of the San Antonio Retail Merchants Association and is listed by Dun and Bradstreet.

If you would like to have the Nationwide Locator perform any of these searches, please write or FAX the information required to perform the search along with the following:

1. Payment in full: check, money order or credit card. If using Visa, MasterCard or American Express, please include your card number, the expiration date, the amount charged and your signature.
2. Your name
3. Address
4. City, State and ZIP
5. Phone number
6. FAX number
7. A self addressed stamped business size envelope.

Please write or FAX the above information to:

The Nationwide Locator   FAX (210) 828-4667
PO Box 39903
San Antonio, Texas 78218

Chapter Eleven

Case Studies

Each section below is an actual case that has been solved. Each heading states the main method used. Each paragraph contains the important details and the actual steps taken to solve the case. This will allow you to see how the information you have has been applied in other situations. If these people have been able to solve their cases, you can solve yours. All names have been changed to protect the privacy of the individuals.

Alumni Group And Address Update

Sally and Scott Jessup were about to celebrate their twentieth wedding anniversary. Sally wanted to find Becky Hunter, who had been Maid of Honor at their wedding. Sally knew Becky's year of birth, but was sure Becky had married since they last saw each other. Sally also knew where Becky lived at the time of the wedding. She called the telephone information operator in that town to find out if there were any families with the name Hunter still living there. There were none, so she called the library and found out that the local high school had a reunion association. She contacted them and they gave her Becky's married name and an address that was a few years old. With this information, she had an Address Update performed, but this failed to show her current address. The report listed former neighbors, so Sally contacted one who knew Becky and her current phone number. Becky and her husband were able to come to the anniversary celebration.

Alumni Group, City Directory And Address Update

Chuck Thompson wished to find his best friend from college, Dennis Brolin. He knew approximately when Dennis was born and the city where he had lived. A search of the city failed to provide any clues. Chuck then contacted the college alumni association. They had an address that was over ten years old. He had a researcher check city directories and old telephone books in that city. The researcher found a more current address that was only five years old. With this address, Chuck had a computer Address Update run. It returned the current address and phone number of Dennis.

Civic Organization

Thelma Simmons needed to find her ex-husband, John. He was several thousands of dollars behind on child support payments. He had moved and she did not know where. The letters she wrote to him were returned with a notation by the Post Office, "NO FORWARDING ADDRESS". She had an Address Update run, but this did not produce a new address. The same was true for a SSN Trace. In both cases, his old address was listed on the computer reports. She contacted the state Parent Locator, but this also was unsuccessful. She contacted his parents but they said they did not know where he had moved. Thelma then contacted the civic organizations in the town where he had lived. She found one organization that he had been a member of, but his membership had been transferred to another city. After she explained the circumstances concerning her search, the organization gave his new address to her.

Criss-Cross And SSN Trace

A collection agency was seeking Louise Dobson for a client. Ms. Dobson was delinquent on a large debt. The agency had her previous address. After the normal means used by this agency to locate missing people failed to produce a current address, they did a computer criss-cross search. They entered Ms. Dobson's name and former address into the computer. They obtained a more current address and her SSN. Even this newer address was not her current one, so they ran an SSN Trace (on another Credit Bureau file) and obtained the most current address for Louise Dobson.

Date Of Birth Search (exact)

Stephen Cross, an estate researcher, was looking for Anthony Smith, an heir to a large estate. The only information available was Anthony's date of birth. There were over six hundred people with that name on the National Telephone Directory. Stephen had the Nationwide Locator run the Date of Birth search with the Anthony's name and date of birth. The file contained only five people with that name who were born on that particular day. On his third telephone call, Stephen located the missing heir.

Date of Birth Search (approximate)

A newspaper was doing a story about an event that happened several years ago. They needed to find Greg McLoud, who was an eye witness to the event. The newspaper knew Greg's home address at the time the event occurred, but nothing more. No one in town knew what had happened to Greg or where he had moved. A computer Address Update did not show a more current address. He was not listed on the National Telephone Directory. A check of the SSA Master Death Index was negative. A check of voter registration files in the courthouse and library was also negative. He did not have a current driver license in the state where he had lived. As a last resort, a Date Of Birth search was made by entering his name and a five year span around his estimated date of birth. This search provided several matching names with their date of birth and city of residence. They were all called and the last one reached was the correct Greg McLoud.

Department of Veterans Affairs

Kevin Buchman needed to locate Michael Shalski. They had served together in the Army during the Korean War. Kevin knew Michael's approximate year of birth. He called the VA. They were able to identify Michael on their computer file and had his current address. Kevin forwarded a letter through the VA and received a reply from his friend within a few weeks.

FAA Pilot License

Mary Morgan wanted to contact her former boyfriend, David O'Neill. David was a pilot and a Captain in the Air Force. She wrote the Air Force World-Wide Locator who told her that he had been discharged. She contacted the VA, but they did not have his address because he had not filed for any VA benefits. Mary then contacted the Federal Aviation Agency (FAA). Since he now had a civilian pilot's license, they were able to give her David's current address.

First Name And Date of Birth

Theresa Washington was searching for her natural mother. Theresa had been adopted and the only information she could obtain was her mother's first name and date of birth.

She contacted the Nationwide Locator and requested a Date of Birth search. It contained the full names of ten women with the same first name and date of birth. Theresa contacted each person on the report and located her mother on the eighth telephone call.

Former Neighbor

Peter Bentson had been friends with Walter Griffin for over 40 years, but hadn't heard from him since 1990. Walter had moved and Peter didn't know his current address. He had a computer Address Update run. It did not give Walter's new address, but it did list several former neighbors. One of the neighbors he called gave him Walter's current address and telephone number.

Military Locator

Nathan Ewing had not seen or heard from his son, Paul in over three years. He knew his son had joined the Army, but had no idea where Paul was stationed. Mr. Ewing contacted everyone who may have heard from his son. No one knew Paul's whereabouts. He then wrote to the Army World-Wide Locator. A week later they sent him Paul's military address.

Military Reunion Group

A high school alumni group had located everyone from their class except the class vice-president, Josh Richardson. The only information they had was his name, a year of birth and that he had served with the 101st Airborne Division in Vietnam. A call to the National Reunion Registry gave them the telephone number of that unit's reunion association. The reunion association had his name, address and telephone number, which they provided.

Name And Date Of Birth

Melinda Flores wanted to locate her brother whom she had not seen in over 40 years. The only identifying information she had was his name, date of birth and that he had lived somewhere in the state of Florida in 1952. She first had a driver license search run for Florida, but his name was not listed. She went to the main library and searched the National Telephone Directory, but again the results were negative. Next Melinda had a Date Of Birth search made. He was listed on this file with an address in Oklahoma. She contacted him immediately and they were soon reunited.

Officers Register And Alumni Group

Jane Martin was recently divorced and wanted to find an old boyfriend that she knew in 1965 while he was in the Army. Andy had been an officer, but she couldn't remember his exact rank. She wasn't even sure of the exact spelling of his last name. She went to her main library and requested the 1965 copy of the Army officers register through the Inter-Library Loan program. This book showed the correct spelling of his name, date of birth, service number and the college he attended. She contacted the college alumni association. The alumni association would not release his address. They did, however, forward a letter she wrote to him. Andy had been divorced for some time. He called her as soon as he got her letter.

Old City Directory

Oscar Padillo wanted to find his brother, Albert, whom he had not seen in over ten years. He wrote to the last known address, but the letter was returned by the post office. There was no forwarding address on file. He called the library in the town where Albert had lived. The librarian checked city directories and old telephone books and discovered a more recent address. Oscar wrote to Albert at this address and again the letter was returned. The label placed on the envelope by the post office stated that the forwarding order had expired as it was over 12 months old. However, the label also provided Albert's current address and the brothers were soon reunited.

Social Security Administration

Ty Suhor's parents divorced almost 15 years ago. Ty had not seen his father since then and wanted to locate him . He had his father's name and SSN, so he hired a private investigator to run all available SSN Traces. His father did not show up on any file. The same was true of the National Telephone Directory. His father's name was not even listed on the VA file. Ty had the SSA forward a letter to his father. His father called as soon as he received Ty's letter.

SSA Master Death Index

Emma Dawson wanted to find her brother whom she had not heard from in 50 years. She went to the Latter Day Saints (Mormon) Family Library in a nearby city and searched the SSA Master Death Index for his name. The index contained his name and his date and place of death. Emma called the information operator for that city and received the phone numbers for her sister-in-law and her nephews.

SSN From The IRS

Claire Riley needed to contact her former spouse, but did not remember his SSN or date of birth. She wrote to the IRS and requested a copy of a joint tax return filed while they were married. It contained his SSN. Claire contacted

the Nationwide Locator and had an SSN Trace run. This
provided his current address.

SSN Master Death Index And Library

Colleen had not seen her father since she was three years
old. She knew he had remarried after he divorced her
mother. Recently, she found out that her father had died,
but that she had a half-sister. She did not know where to
begin her search so she went to the local Latter Day Saints
Family Library. They advised her to run the SSA Master
Death Index. This showed that her father had died in 1991
in Los Altos, CA. She contacted the Los Altos Main
Library which provided a copy of her father's obituary. This
listed her sister's name and home city. She obtained her
sister's telephone number from the telephone assistance
operator. Colleen immediately called her sister. They met a
few weeks later.

State Driver License Search

Tom Davis had not heard from his Uncle Jim for years. The
family believed Jim was dead. The last address they had
was in New York and it was 15 years old. Jim was born on
March 7, 1925. Since Jim was more than 60 years old, Tom
had the SSA Death Index run, but his uncle was not listed.
Tom contacted the Vital Records office in New York state,
but they did not have any information on Uncle Jim. Tom
then contacted the VA because his uncle had been in the
Navy in World War II. The VA did not have a report of
death. Since many people who live in New York often
retire in Florida, Tom had a driver license search made for
the state of Florida. This report provided his uncle's current
address. Tom called and a few months later Uncle Jim was
reunited with the family for Christmas.

Telephone Number Ownership

Valerie Metzger wanted to contact her son, Bill, whom she hadn't seen in over five years. The only contact she had had with him was a collect telephone call from him about six months prior. She looked at the telephone bill that listed his call. It showed the telephone number Bill had called from. Valerie sent this number to the Nationwide Locator and requested a Telephone Number Ownership search. The phone was listed in the name of Samantha Daughtry. Valerie called and talked to Samantha who admitted that she had been Bills's girlfriend. She gave Valerie Bill's current address and telephone number.

Utility Company

Attorney Yvonne Franklin was attempting to locate Donald Cody. Mr. Cody was needed as a witness in a civil trial. Ms. Franklin knew Mr. Cody's place of employment six years ago, and that he was an engineer. The former employer had no record of Donald Cody's new address. The attorney contacted the state regulating agency that licenses engineers. She was told Mr. Cody was last known to be living in Tucson, Arizona about two years ago, but had moved. They did not have his current address. Ms. Franklin checked with the utility company in Tucson and found that his utility deposit refund had been mailed to San Bernardino, California. A call to the telephone information operator provided him with Mr. Cody's current telephone number and address.

Veteran Organization

Hal Smith needed to find Stan Baldwin. Stan owed Hal's business a large sum of money. Stan had moved approximately two years ago and had not given the post office a forwarding address. His neighbors did not know where he had moved. The same was true for all local businesses and civic organizations. The local VFW post said that he was a member, but did not know his new location. Hal then contacted the VFW National Headquarters and they provided Stan's new address.

Voter Registration And SSN Trace

Sue Miller needed to find her uncle, James Travis. James had inherited some property and Sue wanted to make sure he knew about it. No one in the family had seen or heard from James in over ten years. They knew his address at that time, but he no longer lived there. An Address Update search failed to produce a more current address. Sue went to the library in the town where Uncle James last lived and reviewed the county voter registration files. She found her uncle's name, date of birth and SSN. With this information, Sue had a SSN Trace run. They got a hit and she had James current address within 24 hours.

Chapter Twelve

Personal Search
By The Author

The author has performed thousands of successful searches to locate relatives, birth parents, witnesses, friends, etc. He has performed these searches for private investigators, attorneys, television programs, military reunion organizations, relatives and other individuals.

For additional information and fees, contact:

Richard S Johnson   FAX (210) 828-4667
The Nationwide Locator
PO Box 39903
San Antonio, TX 78218

Conclusion

Now that you have read this book, you realize there are many methods available to locate people. It may take more than one attempt to be successful, but if persistent, you will ultimately find the person you are trying to locate. If at this point you have not been successful in your search, you should read the appropriate sections of the book again. Computer searches have proven to be the most successful means to locate anyone. Be sure you understand the different computer searches that are available and make use of them.

If you have any questions or problems concerning information or methods in this book, write the author at the address listed below. We would also appreciate hearing about any successful searches.

Since the information contained in this book may change from time to time, revised editions will be published periodically. If you have any comments that may improve future copies of this book they will certainly be appreciated. Please contact me at the following address:

Richard S. Johnson
The Nationwide Locator
PO Box 39903
San Antonio, TX 78218

There are millions of people in this country who are searching for friends and relatives and do not know how to go about locating them. If you have been helped by this book and were successful in your search, perhaps you would like other people who are searching to know about this book. If this is the case, we strongly encourage you to communicate this information to any or all of the following:

Your friends	Family genealogical
The local library	organizations
Churches	High school reunion groups
Civic organizations	College alumni and reunion
Patriotic organizations	groups
Fraternal organizations	Dear Abby
Veterans groups	Ann Landers
Newspapers	Paul Harvey
	The Oprah Winfrey Show

Appendices

Social Security Number Allocations

This is an explanation of where and when SSN are assigned. This information may assist you in your search.

The **Social Security Administration** (SSA) was formed in 1933. Between 1933 and 1972, SSN were assigned at field offices in each state. The area number identified the state in which the field office was located. Since 1973, SSN have been issued by the SSA central office.

The Social Security number consists of nine (9) digits. The **first three** (3) digits are the area number. The **middle two** (2) digits are the group number. The **last four** (4) digits are the serial number.

EXAMPLE: 123-45-6789

123	45	6789
Area	Group	Serial
No.	No.	No.

Area Number

The area number assigned by the central office identifies the state indicated in the original application.

The chart below shows the first 3 digits (area number) of the Social Security numbers allocated to each state and US possession.

001-003	New Hampshire	212-220 .... Maryland
004-007	Maine	221-222 .... Delaware
008-009	Vermont	223-231, 691-699* .... Virginia
010-034	Massachusetts	232-236 .... West Virginia
035-039	Rhode Island	232, 237-246, 681-690* ....
040-049	Connecticut	.... North Carolina
050-134	New York	247-251, 654-658* .... S Carolina
135-158	New Jersey	252-260, 667-675* .... Georgia
159-211	Pennsylvania	261-267, 589-595 .... Florida

268-302	Ohio	516-517	Montana
303-317	Indiana	518-519	Idaho
318-361	Illinois	520	Wyoming
362-386	Michigan	521-524, 650-653*	Colorado
387-399	Wisconsin	525, 585, 648-649*	
400-407	Kentucky		New Mexico
408-415, 756-763*	Tennessee	526-527, 600-601	Arizona
416-424	Alabama	528-529, 646-647*	Utah
425-428, 587, 588*, 752-755*		530, 680*	Nevada
	Mississippi	531- 539	Washington
429-432, 676-679*	Arkansas	540-544	Oregon
433-439, 659-665*	Louisiana	545-573, 602-626*	California
440-448	Oklahoma	574	Alaska
449-467, 627-645	Texas	575-576, 750-751*	Hawaii
468-477	Minnesota	577-579	District of Columbia
478-485	Iowa	580	Virgin Islands
486-500	Missouri	580-584, 596-599	Puerto Rico
501-502	North Dakota	586	Guam
503-504	South Dakota	586	American Samoa
505-508	Nebraska	586	Philippine Islands
509-515	Kansas	700-728**	Railroad Board

* New areas (prefixes) allocated but not yet issued.

** 700-728 RRB (Railroad Board). Issuance of these numbers to railroad employees was discontinued July 1, 1963.

NOTE: The same area number, when shown more than once means that certain numbers have been transferred from one state to another, or that an area number has been divided for use among certain geographic locations.

Area numbers range from 001 through 587, 589 through 649, and 700 through 728. Social Security numbers containing area numbers other than these are invalid.

Prior to converting from service numbers to Social Security numbers as a means of identification, the military assigned dummy Social Security numbers to individuals who did not have them. These dummy area numbers range from 900 through 999 and appear on some military orders and unit rosters in the late 1960s and early 1970s. These dummy numbers were later replaced with valid Social Security numbers.

Group Number

The **first three** (3) digits denote the area (or state) of the SSN. Within each area, group numbers (**middle two** (2) digits) are allocated. These numbers range from 01 to 99 but are not assigned in consecutive order. For administrative reasons, group numbers issued first consist of the odd numbers from 01 through 09 and then even numbers from 10 through 98, within each area number allocated to a state. After all even numbers in group 98 of a particular area have been issued, the even numbers 02 through 08 are used, followed by odd numbers 11 through 99 as shown:

ODD	EVEN	EVEN	ODD
01, 03, 05, 07,09	10 to 98	02, 04, 06, 08	11 to 99

The chart below shows the highest group number allocated for each area number as of September 1, 1994.

001-003......... 86	212-220......... 41	303-309......... 15
004-006......... 94	221-222......... 84	310-317......... 13
007............... 92	223-226......... 71	318-336......... 90
008-019......... 78	227-231......... 69	337-361......... 88
020-034......... 76	232-236......... 41	362-375......... 17
035-039......... 62	237-239......... 79	376-386......... 15
040-047......... 92	240-246......... 77	387-393......... 13
048-049......... 90	247-248......... 95	394-399......... 11
050-124......... 82	249-251......... 93	400-404......... 47
125-134......... 80	252............... 91	405-407......... 45
135-146......... 96	253-260......... 89	408-415......... 75
147-158......... 94	261-267......... 99	416-417......... 43
159-206......... 74	268-298......... 96	418-424......... 41
207-211......... 72	299-302......... 94	425-428......... 77

429-430......... 87	512-515......... 08	588................. 00
431-432......... 85	516-517......... 27	589-595......... 43
433-436......... 89	518-519......... 45	596-597......... 44
437-439......... 87	520................. 33	598-599......... 42
440-442......... 06	521-523......... 93	600-601......... 41
443-448......... 04	524................. 91	602-603......... 76
449-467......... 99	525-529......... 99	604-626......... 74
468................. 29	530................. 81	627-639......... 42
469-477......... 27	531-535......... 31	640-645......... 40
478................. 29	536-539......... 29	646-647......... 20
479-482......... 23	540-544......... 43	648-649......... 03
483-485......... 21	545-573......... 99	650-699......... 00
486-500......... 08	574................. 15	700-723......... 18
501................. 21	575................. 69	724................. 28
502................. 19	576................. 67	725-726......... 18
503................. 25	577-579......... 25	727................. 10
504................. 23	580................. 29	728................. 14
505-507......... 33	581-585......... 99	750-763......... 00
508................. 31	586................. 19	
509-511......... 11	587................. 75	

Serial Number

Within each group, the serial numbers (last four (4) digits of the Social Security number) run consecutively from 0001 through 9999.

Freedom Of Information Act Request

This is a sample letter for contacting the armed forces and federal agencies only.

Date

Agency Head or FOIA Officer
Name of agency or agency component
Address

Dear _____ :

Under the **Freedom of Information Act**, 5 USC. subsection 552, I am requesting access to, or copies of (identify the records as clearly and specifically as possible).

If there are any fees for copying or searching for the records, please let me know before you fill my request. (Or, please supply the records without informing me of the cost if the fees do not exceed $___ , which I agree to pay.)

Optional: I am requesting this information because (state the reason(s) if you think it will help you obtain the information).

If you deny all or any part of this request, please cite each specific exemption you think justifies your refusal to release the information and notify me of appeal procedures available under the law.

Optional: If you have any questions about handling this request, you may telephone me at (home phone) or at (office phone).

Sincerely,

Your Name
Address

Standard Form 180

REQUEST PERTAINING TO MILITARY RECORDS

Please read instructions on the reverse. If more space is needed, use plain paper.

PRIVACY ACT OF 1974 COMPLIANCE INFORMATION. The following information is provided in accordance with 5 U.S.C. 552a(e)(3) and applies to this form. Authority for collection of the information is 44 U.S.C. 2907, 3101 and 3103, and E.O. 9397 of November 22, 1943. Disclosure of the information is voluntary. The principal purpose of the information is to assist the facility servicing the records in locating and verifying the correctness of the requested records or information to answer your inquiry. Routine uses of the information as established and published in accordance with 5 U.S.C.a(e)(4)(D)

include the transfer of relevant information to appropriate Federal, State, local or foreign agencies for use in civil, criminal, or regulatory investigations or prosecution in addition, this form will be filed with the appropriate military records and may be transferred along with the record to another agency in accordance with the routine uses established by the agency which maintains the record. If the requested information is not provided, it may not be possible to service your inquiry.

SECTION I — INFORMATION NEEDED TO LOCATE RECORDS *(Furnish as much as possible)*

1. NAME USED DURING SERVICE *(Last, first, and middle)*	2. SOCIAL SECURITY NO.	3. DATE OF BIRTH	4. PLACE OF BIRTH

5. ACTIVE SERVICE, PAST AND PRESENT   *(For an effective records search, it is important that ALL service be shown below)*

BRANCH OF SERVICE *(Also, show last organization, if known)*	DATES OF ACTIVE SERVICE		Check one		SERVICE NUMBER DURING THIS PERIOD
	DATE ENTERED	DATE RELEASED	OFFI-CER	EN-LISTED	

6. RESERVE SERVICE, PAST OR PRESENT   *If "none," check here* ▶ ☐

a. BRANCH OF SERVICE	b. DATES OF MEMBERSHIP		c. Check one		d. SERVICE NUMBER DURING THIS PERIOD
	FROM	TO	OFFI-CER ☐	EN-LISTED ☐	

7. NATIONAL GUARD MEMBERSHIP *(Check one):*   ☐ a. ARMY   ☐ b. AIR FORCE   ☐ c. NONE

d. STATE	e. ORGANIZATION	f. DATES OF MEMBERSHIP		g. Check one		h. SERVICE NUMBER DURING THIS PERIOD
		FROM	TO	OFFI-CER ☐	EN-LISTED ☐	

8. IS SERVICE PERSON DECEASED ☐ YES ☐ NO *If "yes," enter date of death.*	9. IS (WAS) INDIVIDUAL A MILITARY RETIREE OR FLEET RESERVIST ☐ YES ☐ NO

SECTION II — REQUEST

1. EXPLAIN WHAT INFORMATION OR DOCUMENTS YOU NEED; OR, CHECK ITEM 2, OR, COMPLETE ITEM 3					2. IF YOU ONLY NEED A STATEMENT OF SERVICE check here ☐

3. LOST SEPARATION DOCUMENT REPLACEMENT REQUEST *(Complete a or b, and c.)*

☐	a. REPORT OF SEPARATION *(DD Form 214 or equivalent)*	YEAR ISSUED	This contains information normally needed to determine eligibility for benefits. It may be furnished only to the veteran, the surviving next of kin, or to a representative with veteran's signed release (Item 5 of this form)
☐	b. DISCHARGE CERTIFICATE	YEAR ISSUED	This shows only the date and character at discharge. It is of little value in determining eligibility for benefits. It may be issued only to veterans discharged honorably or under honorable conditions; or, if deceased, to the surviving spouse.
c. EXPLAIN HOW SEPARATION DOCUMENT WAS LOST			

4. EXPLAIN PURPOSE FOR WHICH INFORMATION OR DOCUMENTS ARE NEEDED	6. REQUESTER
	a. IDENTIFICATION *(check appropriate box)* ☐ Same person identified in Section I ☐ Surviving spouse ☐ Next of kin *(relationship)* _____ ☐ Other *(specify)* _____
	b. SIGNATURE *(see instruction 3 on reverse side)* DATE OF REQUEST

5. RELEASE AUTHORIZATION, IF REQUIRED *(Read instruction 3 on reverse side)*	7. Please type or print clearly — COMPLETE RETURN ADDRESS
I hereby authorize release of the requested information/documents to the person indicated at right (item 7).	Name, number and street, city, State and ZIP code
VETERAN SIGN HERE ▶ *(If signed by other than veteran show relationship to veteran.)*	TELEPHONE NO. *(include area code)* ▶

INSTRUCTIONS

1. Information needed to locate records. Certain identifying information is necessary to determine the location of an individual's record of military service. Please give careful consideration to and answer each item on this form. If you do not have and cannot obtain the information for an item, show "NA," meaning the information is "not available." Include as much of the requested information as you can. This will help us to give you the best possible service.

2. Charges for service. A nominal fee is charged for certain types of service. In most instances service fees cannot be determined in advance. If your request involves a service fee you will be notified as soon as that determination is made.

3. Restrictions on release of information. Information from records of military personnel is released subject to restrictions imposed by the military departments consistent with the provisions of the Freedom of Information Act of 1967 (as amended in 1974) and the Privacy Act of 1974. A service person has access to almost any information contained in his own record. The next of kin, if the veteran is deceased, and Federal officers for official purposes, are authorized to receive information from a military service or medical record only as specified in the above cited Acts. Other requesters must have the release authorization, in item 5 of the form, signed by the veteran or, if deceased, by the next of kin. Employers

and others needing proof of military service are expected to accept the information shown on documents issued by the Armed Forces at the time a service person is separated.

4. Location of military personnel records. The various categories of military personnel records are described in the chart below. For each category there is a code number which indicates the address at the bottom of the page to which this request should be sent. For each military service there is a note explaining approximately how long the records are held by the military service before they are transferred to the National Personnel Records Center, St. Louis. Please read these notes carefully and make sure you send your inquiry to the right address. Please note especially that the record is not sent to the National Personnel Records Center as long as the person retains any sort of reserve obligation, whether drilling or non-drilling.

(If the person has two or more periods of service within the same branch, send your request to the office having the record for the last period of service.)

5. Definitions for abbreviations used below:
NPRC – National Personnel Records Center   PERS – Personnel Records
TDRL – Temporary Disability Retirement List   MED – Medical Records

SERVICE	NOTE: (See paragraph 4 above.)	CATEGORY OF RECORDS	WHERE TO WRITE ADDRESS CODE	▼
AIR FORCE (USAF)	Except for TDRL, and general officers retired with pay, Air Force records are transferred to NPRC from Code 1, 90 days after separation and from Code 2, 150 days after separation.	Active members (includes National Guard on active duty in the Air Force), TDRL, and general officers retired with pay		1
		Reserve, retired reservist in nonpay status, current National Guard officers not on active duty in Air Force, and National Guard released from active duty in Air Force.		2
		Current National Guard enlisted not on active duty in Air Force.		13
		Discharged, deceased, and retired with pay.		14
COAST GUARD (USCG)	Coast Guard officer and enlisted records are transferred to NPRC 7 months after separation.	Active, reserve, and TDRL members.		3
		Discharged, deceased, and retired members (see next item).		14
		Officers separated before 1/1/29 and enlisted personnel separated before 1/1/15.		6
MARINE CORPS (USMC)	Marine Corps records are transferred to NPRC between 6 and 9 months after separation.	Active, TDRL, and Selected Marine Corps Reserve members.		4
		Individual Ready Reserve and Fleet Marine Corps Reserve members.		5
		Discharged, deceased, and retired members (see next item).		14
		Members separated before 1/1/1905.		6
ARMY (USA)	Army records are transferred to NPRC as follows: Active Army and Individual Ready Reserve Control Groups: About 80 days after separation. U.S. Army Reserve Troop Unit personnel: About 120 to 180 days after separation.	Reserve, living retired members, retired general officers, and active duty records of current National Guard members who performed service in the U.S. Army before 7/1/72.*		7
		Active officers (including National Guard on active duty in the U.S. Army)		8
		Active enlisted (including National Guard on active duty in the U.S. Army) and enlisted TDRL.		9
		Current National Guard officers not on active duty in the U.S. Army.		12
		Current National Guard enlisted not on active duty in the U.S. Army.		13
		Discharged and deceased members (see next item).		14
		Officers separated before 7/1/17 and enlisted separated before 11/1/12.		6
		Officers and warrant officers TDRL.		8
NAVY (USN)	Navy records are transferred to NPRC 6 months after retirement or complete separation.	Active members (including reserves on duty) – PERS and MED		10
		Discharged, deceased, retired (with and without pay) less than six months.	PERS ONLY	10
		TDRL, drilling and nondrilling reservists	MED ONLY	11
		Discharged, deceased, retired (with and without pay) more than six months (see next item) – PERS & MED		14
		Officers separated before 1/1/03 and enlisted separated before 1/1/1886 – PERS and MED		6

*Code 12 applies to active duty records of current National Guard officers who performed service in the U.S. Army after 6/30/72.
Code 13 applies to active duty records of current National Guard enlisted members who performed service in the U.S. Army after 6/30/72.

	ADDRESS LIST OF CUSTODIANS (BY CODE NUMBERS SHOWN ABOVE) – Where to write / send this form for each category of records					
1	Air Force Manpower and Personnel Center Military Personnel Records Division Randolph AFB, TX 78150-6001	**5**	Marine Corps Reserve Support Center 10950 El Monte Overland Park, KS 66211-1408	**8**	USA MILPERCEN ATTN: DAPC-MSR 200 Stovall Street Alexandria, VA 22332-0400	**12**	Army National Guard Personnel Center Columbia Pike Office Building 5600 Columbia Pike Falls Church, VA 22041
2	Air Reserve Personnel Center Denver, CO 80280-5000	**6**	Military Archives Division National Archives and Records Administration Washington, DC 20408	**9**	Commander U.S. Army Enlisted Records and Evaluation Center Ft. Benjamin Harrison, IN 46249-5301	**13**	The Adjutant General (of the appropriate State, DC, or Puerto Rico)
3	Commandant U.S. Coast Guard Washington, DC 20593-0001	**7**	Commander U.S. Army Reserve Personnel Center ATTN: DARP-PAS 9700 Page Boulevard St. Louis, MO 63132-5200	**10**	Commander Naval Military Personnel Command ATTN: NMPC-036 Washington, DC 20370-5036	**14**	National Personnel Records Center (Military Personnel Records) 9700 Page Boulevard St. Louis, MO 63132
4	Commandant of the Marine Corps (Code MMRB-10) Headquarters, U.S. Marine Corps Washington, DC 20380-0001			**11**	Naval Reserve Personnel Center New Orleans, LA 70146-5000		

STANDARD FORM 180 BACK (Rev. 1-86)

Military Records Authorization

Military Information Enterprises, Inc. can acquire records rapidly from the **National Personnel Records Center** and the **Army Reserve Personnel Center** in St. Louis, MO. All requests are properly prepared and hand carried to the appropriate Center, thus assuring that you will receive the records you need in the most rapid manner possible. The following records may be obtained:

1. Certified copies of **Report of Separation (DD-214)** for anyone discharged or retired from any of the armed forces and army reservists who have been separated from active duty. Fee is $50.00. Allow four to six weeks for delivery.

2. A copy of the **complete military personnel and medical records** (every item in the file is copied) of an individual may be provided to the veteran or his next of kin if the veteran is deceased. Fee is $100.00. This includes records of individuals who are retired from any armed forces, most individuals who are discharged and have no reserve obligation for all branches and current members of the Army reserve. Copies of military records of individuals on active duty, current members of the Army National Guard and Air National Guard, current members of the Navy, Marine and Air Force reserves cannot be obtained. These records are not at St. Louis. MO.*

> **NOTE:** Requests for DD-214 and military records are made with the authorization form shown on the next page. It must be completed and signed by the veteran or his next of kin, if deceased.

3. Certified copies of **complete military personnel and medical records** may also be obtained for attorneys and

private investigators in four to six weeks **for court cases**. A court order signed by a federal or state judge is required. A sample of how the court order should be worded will be mailed or faxed upon request. The fee for this service is $200.00. *

4. **Organizational records** can also be obtained. Write for details.

> In July 1973, a fire at the NPRC destroyed 75-80% of the records for the Army (discharged from 1912 to 1960) and Air Force (H through Z discharged 1947 through 1964). Some of these records have been partially reconstructed and others were only partially destroyed. An exact determination of their condition can only be made by reviewing the records.

All fees are for research and in the event the records requested are not available or have been destroyed, the fee is not refundable. All requests must be prepaid and all information concerning the request should be included. All orders are shipped by first class mail but may be shipped by Federal Express for an additional fee of $10.00. Checks should be made payable to Military Information Enterprises, Inc. (not affiliated with the federal government) or you may make payment by VISA, MasterCard or AMEX. For additional information or to order records, mail or FAX authorization to:

Military Information Enterprises, Inc.
PO Box 340081   (210) 828-4667 FAX
Ft Sam Houston, TX 78234

Military Records Authorization

I request and authorize that representatives of Military Information Enterprises, Inc. be allowed to review my Military Service Personnel and Medical Records in the same manner as if I presented myself for this purpose. I specifically authorize the National Personnel Records Center, St. Louis, MO, or other custodians of my military records, to release to Military Information Enterprises, Inc. a complete copy of my military personnel and related medical records.

I am willing that a photocopy and or FAX of this authorization be considered as effective and valid as the original.

Signature _____ date _____

If veteran is deceased, date of death_____ and relationship _____

Instructions: Type or print this authorization.

Name _____
        Last   First   Middle initial

_____
        Street address   Apt. #

_____
        City   State   ZIP

Social Security number _____

Date of birth_____ Place of birth _____

Telephone number _____

Service number _____ Branch of service _____

Dates of service _____ Rank _____

Current military status ( )reserve, ( ) retired,
( ) separated with Army reserve obligation, ( ) none

Please obtain ( ) DD-214, ( ) complete military records,
( ) other _____

Enclosed is ( ) check, ( ) money order, charge my ( ) Visa
( ) MasterCard ( ) AMEX for $ _____

Card number _____ Expir. date _____

Signature _____

Address of where records are to be sent, if different from above _

_____

Glossary

Address

The place where one lives or works; consists of name of the street, house or building number, apartment or suite number, city, state and zip code. A mailing address may be a post office box.

Alias

A fictitious name assumed by an individual.

Archives

The place where historical documents are stored. The place where documents are kept.

Armed Forces

The armed forces are composed of the Air Force, Army, Coast Guard, Marine Corps and the Navy.

Birth Certificate

An official document issued by a government agency that indicates the date and place of birth and the name of an individual. Names of the parents and hospital are usually listed.

Census

An official count of the population in a geographical area. It also collects information about the people such as age, sex, income, etc. Census are conducted by the appropriate government agencies periodically.

Civil Service Employee

An employee of the government who is not a member of the armed forces. This applies to federal, state and local governments.

Computer Search

A search made of a database accessed by computer.

Credit Report

A report of an individual's credit history to include records of commercial and financial accounts.

Database/File
A collection of information; may be maintained and accessed by computer.

Death Certificate
An official document issued by a government agency confirming the date, place and cause of an individual's death. May also include marital status, address at time of death, informants name, veteran status and survivors.

Driver License
A permit to operate a motor vehicle, normally issued by each state government. A license may contain an individual's name, address, physical description and the permit number or SSN.

Fair Credit Reporting Act
A federal law created to protect the credit information of an individual. Only businesses with a valid reason may obtain credit information.

Freedom Of Information Act
The federal law requiring US government executive branch agencies and the armed forces to release information to the public upon request, unless exempted by privacy or national security reasons.

Genealogical Library
A library that specializes in family history information.

Hit
Successful results of a computer search; e.g., obtaining a name and correct address after entering a SSN.

Identifying Information
Information used to identify and locate someone such as name, SSN, service number, date of birth, ship, unit or former unit of assignment.

Legal Name
The name on a person's birth certificate and other government records and documents.

Locator Service

A company that locates missing people from information contained in records and databases.

Merchant Marine

The civilian commercial fleet.

Merchant Mariner

An individual who is employed as a seaman on a commercial ship. Not a member of the military service.

Military Locator

The office on each base or post that has the names and units of assignment of all military personnel at that installation. They will provide this information to anyone who requests it. All armed forces also operate world-wide locators.

National Archives

The depositories of historical documents of the federal government. The National Personnel Records Center is part of the Archives.

Newspaper Archives

A collection of newspapers that were previously published. Many archives have copies from the first date of publication to the present date. Some are kept on microfilm. Some may be kept in the public libraries.

Open Records Act

The laws outlining the information that may be released from official records maintained by state and local government agencies.

Privacy Act

The federal law designed to protect an individual's constitutional right to privacy. The law also provides disclosure to an individual of information the federal government maintains on that individual.

Researcher

An individual who obtains information from libraries, archives, government agencies, private businesses and other sources.

Service Number
The unique number assigned to an individual who served in the armed forces, either on active duty, the reserves or National Guard. This number never had more than eight digits. Some numbers had suffixes and prefixes that were letters. Service numbers were used from World War I to 1974.

Social Security Number
The unique nine digit number assigned to citizens of the United States by the Social Security Administration. In reality, this number is the national identity number.

Subject
The missing person the searcher is attempting to find.

The Uniformed Services
The Uniformed Services are composed of the armed forces, the Public Health Service, and the National Oceanic and Atmospheric Administration.

VA Claim Number
The number assigned by the VA when a veteran makes a claim for benefits. Since 1973, this number is the veteran's Social Security number.

Veteran
A person who has served on active duty in one or more of the armed forces.

Vital Records
Birth and death certificates, marriage licenses, divorce and annulment decrees.

Index

-A-

-B-

-C-

-U-

-V-

Notes

Notes

How To Locate Anyone Who Is Or Has Been In The Military:

Armed Forces Locator Guide

The author, Lt. Col. Richard S. Johnson, is the foremost expert in the nation on locating people with a military connection. Over 65,000 copies of this book have been sold. Users of this book have located thousands of people. The 1995 edition has been completely revised and expanded to 288 pages. The foreword is provided by General William C. Westmoreland.

> **This book contains directories of:**
> All Military Installations in the US
> All Base/Post Locators in the US
> Army, Air Force and Fleet Post Offices
> US Navy and Coast Guard Ships
> Military and Veterans Organizations
> Military Unit Reunion Associations

Here is some of the valuable information covered in this unique book:

★ How to obtain unit of assignment, home address and telephone number of any member of the Army, Navy, Air Force, Marine Corps, Coast Guard, the Reserve Components, and National Guard.

★ How to locate a current, former or retired member of the Armed Forces or Reserve Components.

★ How to locate any of 27 million veterans.

★ How to obtain ship or unit histories.

★ How anyone may obtain copies of official military personnel records or current, former or deceased military members.

How To Investigate By Computer by Ralph D. Thomas. A manual of the new investigative technology that gives you the sources and teaches you to investigate by computer. Learn about hard-to-find sources of information and how to access them. 102 pages **$39.95**

The following books by BRB Publications are available:

The Sourcebook Of Federal Courts, US District And Bankruptcy The definitive guide to searching for case information at the local level within the federal court system. Provides complete information on how to obtain criminal and civil court records and bankruptcy files from federal courts. 672 pages **$33.95**

The Sourcebook Of County/Asset/Lien Records A national guide to all county/city government agencies where real estate transactions, UCC financing statement and federal/state tax liens are recorded. 1995 edition 448 pages **$29.95**

The MVR Book Motor Service Guide A national reference detailing and summarizing, in practical terms, the description, access procedures, regulations and privacy restrictions of driver and vehicle records in all states. Check this book before attempting to locate people through state driver license and MVR offices. 1995 edition 256 pages **$19.95**

The Sourcebook Of State Public Records This book explains how to obtain information at the state level for business records, liens and security interest records (UCC), criminal records, workers compensation and vital records, MVR, occupational licensing, and business names and permits. 304 pages **$29.95**

Order Form
MIE Publishing
PO Box 5143
Burlington, NC 27216
1-800-937-2133

We Accept Government Purchase Orders.

Publication	Price	Num	Amt
Find Anyone *FAST*	$14.95		
How To Locate Anyone Who Is Or Has Been In The Military	$19.95		
Other books desired:			

TOTAL: $ _____

North Carolina orders please add 6% Sales Tax. $ _____

Postage and Handling $ __4.05

Please add $1.00 for each additional book. $ _____

Consult Publisher for International Mail Prices.

Total Amount Enclosed: $ _____

Visa, MasterCard, American Express Card Number:
_____ Expiration Date __ / __ /__

Signature _____

Name: _____

Street/Apt no: _____

City/State/Zip: _____

Telephone: (___)_____

Please remit entire order form.